To Req,

s,

Dave.

MISSING THE CUT

THE HIGHS AND LOWS OF A GOLF PRO
ON THE EDGE OF THE BIG TIME

David Thorp

authorHOUSE®

AuthorHouse™
1663 Liberty Drive, Suite 200
Bloomington, IN 47403
www.authorhouse.com
Phone: 1-800-839-8640

First published by AuthorHouse 6/24/2008

ISBN: 978-1-4343-9350-0 (sc)

Printed in the United States of America
Bloomington, Indiana

This book is printed on acid-free paper.

PROLOGUE

The first golf shot I ever hit was at Roundhay Municipal golf course in Leeds with a three-wood. This in itself was unusual, but when the ball went up in the air and quite a long way I knew this was something I could be really good at. That first swing of a club in 1966 would be the start of a life long obsession with golf, one that would see me experience the kind of highs and lows that only professional sport can bring. This is my story of skill, frustration, success, failure…and just missing out on the big time.

CONTENTS

01

THIS KID COULD BE GOOD

1966 – AGE 12

I had always been a good natural sportsman, growing up in Leeds, excelling at football and cricket, fascinated by the challenge and amazed by the skill of top players.

Golf was a game I was yet to discover, even though I had lived almost next door to the old Moor Allerton Golf Club. A school friend, Martin Lynch, had a grandfather who worked at Roundhay Municipal golf course. He suggested that the two of us might have a golf lesson together at Roundhay. One February morning along we went and had a session with the assistant professional. The teacher's name escapes me, but I do remember striking the ball with that old wooden headed club. This game could be fun!

I had at least one more lesson at Roundhay, before the family - Mother, Father, three-year-old brother Andrew and myself emigrated to Montreal, Canada in March 1966. Dad's business career had more than its fair share of highs and lows, and this major move was intended to help make a fresh start. He had started as an accountant, but before long branched out into the building business as "Thorp of Leeds" and succeeded in constructing what seemed to be a large number of houses in Leeds and Knaresborough.

Soon there was also a haulage business based near Elland Road with a fleet of lorries carrying the Thorp name. Maybe the expansion had come too quickly, but for whatever reason the empire came tumbling down and soon we were living in a much smaller house and on the verge of moving to Montreal. Our migration to Canada was aided by a distant relative, known as Uncle Bud. He was a vice-president of Rolls-Royce in Canada and a pillar of the community.

I was desperate to develop my new golf skills, but was lacking one crucial thing – clubs! Being a newcomer to the game, I didn't yet own any, but my Canadian Uncle Bud came to the rescue and kindly gave me an old set of Spalding Top-Flite irons and Bobby Jones woods with brown shafts in a canvas bag. And that's where it all began.

A lot of my new school friends liked golf, and once the spring thaw had set in we used to hit balls around a strangely abandoned golf course next to our school. Soon I started to play at Dorval Municipal course, a flat, tree-lined nine-hole course running alongside the busy international airport. I bought my first instructional book by Sam Snead, with flip-over pages of his swing, which I tried to copy exactly. There were lots of kids to play with at Dorval, including my pal Paul Vickers, who was my regular partner. I gradually upgraded my clubs one by one at the local department store. Sticking with the Spalding brand, I began making up a set of Kro-Flites with shiny steel shafts and leather grips. I also developed a liking for the Spalding Dot ball, and would sometimes buy one for competitions if sufficient funds were available. Amazingly, I got down to 10 handicap that summer, although retrospectively, I wonder how genuine that was!

Somehow I managed to fit cricket, football and fishing - as well as going to school - into my busy schedule, and was selected to play in an inter-provincial boys cricket tournament in Vancouver on Canada's Pacific west coast during the summer holidays. This was a long way from home for a 13 year-old, but off I went and spent a week at the University of B.C. I didn't play very well but it was a great adventure and made me feel even more at home in the sporting arena.

1967–AGE 13

Heavy snowfalls mean there is no golf during the winter in Montreal so I had to wait until spring to play again. In the meantime, we had moved the short distance from Dorval to Beaconsfield, and I had also switched schools.

There was a pay and play course, Beaurepaire, at the end of our street, and a little farther away, a high-class, old-style country club, Beaconsfield, which had twice hosted the Canadian Open. The first was in 1946, when George Fazio triumphed and again in 1956 when Doug Sanders, an amateur at the time, became champion.

Still playing at Dorval, and sometimes at Beaurepaire, I started to caddy at Beaconsfield. It was exactly like the club portrayed in the film "Caddyshack", complete with mad caddymaster. Caddies were allowed to play very early on Monday mornings, a privilege I took full advantage of, splashing through the dew! This was my first experience of a proper golf course. After watching Billy Casper win the Canadian Open on television at Montreal Municipal I persuaded my Dad to take me there to play. I enjoyed trying to emulate the Pros, and thought I might one day compete at the top level.

Expo '67 was taking place at this time, and I was lucky enough to make several visits to the exciting world fair. An international football tournament was held as part of the celebrations and England, as newly crowned world champions, were taking part. I saw them beat Mexico 3-0 and then once again prevail over West Germany 3-2 to win the final. It was great to see several of the team from '66 including Gordon Banks, Jack Charlton and Alan Ball.

Initially, my Dad had been working for an accountancy firm in Montreal. For some reason this didn't work out and he moved to another company. He seemed unable to settle into the routine of a daily commute to the office and spent increasing amounts of time at home suffering from stress. I think his main problem was having to work for somebody else after having run his own sizeable business. It is difficult to take orders when you are used to giving them.

In August we went on a trip back to England for a few weeks holiday, during which I played Roundhay with school-friend John Ingham, scoring a creditable 79. Then it was back to Montreal with my father (Mother and Andrew stayed in England) for what was to be only a couple of months before returning to England permanently.

During this time, on October 9th. to be precise, I played with Paul Vickers at Summerlea C.C. in Montreal, a high class course where Paul's uncle was a member. Summerlea had also held the national Open in 1935. This was to be my last round of golf for several months. My father was now having serious financial and mental problems and decided it wouldn't work out for him in Canada, and as the winter chill set in, we rejoined the rest of the family in Leeds, staying for several weeks in the small house of my Uncle Joe and Auntie Maureen with my three young cousins.

The year and nine months spent in Montreal had been tremendously exciting for me. My golf, football and cricket had all come on well and my French had improved by leaps and bounds!

November found me back in Leeds, re-installed in my old school, St. Thomas Aquinas, in the fourth form. The family was in disarray, I didn't seem to have any clubs (the cost of transportation from Canada must have been prohibitive), and I had to get a paper round to earn some money. At least it wasn't as cold as Montreal, but England in the sixties seemed a drab place compared to the bright and affluent Canada.

1968–AGE 14

Over the winter, I played lots of football but no golf. One day, after school, I went to play at Temple Newsam municipal, hired some clubs and bought an old five iron. I was determined to get back into golf and practised in fields with my one and only club.

Living in a rented flat above some shops in Alwoodley, I was close to the wealthy Jewish club, Moor Allerton. My friends and

I thought it would be a good idea to go caddying there, which we did and found it quite lucrative. We also discovered that, just before dark, we could play on the bottom end of the course undisturbed.

I went down to Alwoodley Golf Club a few times, hired clubs and paid a green fee. At the time this wasn't too expensive, but I hate to think what it would cost today. In fact, I very much doubt that a junior would be allowed to that these days. I enjoyed it, and in my naivety, didn't realise just what a great course it was. Spring arrived and so did my clubs, finally getting shipped from Canada with other family possessions. The pro at Alwoodley was Ian Duncan, whose father George had won The Open in 1920. Ian was very helpful, arranging a holiday job for me assisting the greenstaff, which meant I could also play and practise there.

Now that I had some clubs again, Ian advised me to join Moortown Golf Club, as Alwoodley didn't have many juniors. So, in the summer of 1968 that's exactly what I did and at the tender age of 15 years old I started with the 10 handicap I had previously held in Canada. Like its neighbour Alwoodley, Moortown had been designed by the renowned Dr. Alistair MacKenzie. The club had hosted the 1929 Ryder Cup, in which the British team, led by Ian Duncan's father George, was victorious. I was incredibly lucky to play my early golf on such great courses.

Somehow, I got entered in the 1968 British Boys Championship at St. Annes Old Links in August. To say I was inexperienced for this event is a vast understatement! I had never played a links course, in fact I had never played in a proper golf tournament before, but I was full of confidence and undaunted.

While it wasn't the coolest way to make my first trip into competitive golf, I went over to St. Annes with my Grandma, staying in a local guesthouse! I loved the course in practice, and was more than ready for the first round. Unfortunately my opponent failed to show. A bye saw me through to round two.

Next day the weather turned nasty, and I just couldn't handle the driving rain and wind. My Spalding Kro-Flite clubs with leather grips became as slippery as wet fish and at least once a club came flying out of my hands! Having no waterproofs or bag hood meant I was totally unprepared for the conditions. We must have stayed on for the week because I remember watching the final in which Steven Evans beat Kim Dabson. It had been valuable experience.

Later that summer I played in a junior event at Oakdale and had games at Wetherby and Knaresborough. My golf knowledge was growing.

1969-AGE 15

That winter we moved back to Gledhow, an area of Leeds where we had lived previously. Nearby was a playing field used by the police, but that didn't put me off! I used to practice target golf like on ITV's Saturday afternoon game-show from John Jacobs Sandown Park driving range. It was quite a bad winter, and I spent a lot of time reading about golf and watching any tournaments that were shown on TV. "The Big Three" stands out in my memory with Henry Longhurst's commentary.

The freeze meant that Moortown was closed for six weeks in early New Year, and I couldn't wait to get out again. In fact I was so keen that the assistant Alan had to fetch me off the course when I jumped the gun and went out to play before the course had officially re-opened!

I was having a great time with my football at the time, my career peaking that spring when our St Thomas Aquinas team won the Leeds Schools Cup 1-0 in the final at Elland Road, a proud moment for a lifetime Leeds United supporter. I was selected to play for Northern England Boys against West Germany in an evening match at Barnsley. I wasn't impressed by having to spend the whole match on the bench, but it was still exciting to be involved. Subsequently I seemed to get overlooked after a game with Leeds United juniors at Elland Road, but again I enjoyed the buzz of top level sport.

Moortown's pro at that time, and for many subsequent years, was Bryon Hutchinson, with assistants Ian Wright, Alan Smith and later Don Sterling. I used to hang around the shop and putting green a lot, much as juniors have always done, and was a nuisance to them I'm sure. I did buy my first good putter from Bryon, a Golden Goose, which I then traded in for a Slazenger Jack Nicklaus Ping Anser. If only I had kept that old Ping! They are now highly collectable.

I had managed to buy some second-hand Wilson Staff woods by this time, but my irons were not quite up to scratch. Ian Duncan was kind enough to get me a new set of Slazenger + Jack Nicklaus, two to sand wedge with stiff steel shafts. He not only sold them to me at trade price, but also allowed me to pay by instalments. That's what I call a deal! The new clubs made a massive difference and allowed my fast-improving game to produce results.

We had the Brabazon Trophy, one of the top amateur events, at Moortown in 1969 and, keen to get involved, I joined Jim Buckley and Kim Dabson for a practice round. This was the first time I had played with very good players. Michael Bonallack tied with Peter Tupling, and then beat him in an 18 hole play-off, which I watched. I was amazed that with Bonallack's poor looking swing and strange putting style - reminiscent of a giraffe bending over to drink - he could beat Tupling, who looked much better to my young eyes. Tupling was much longer than Bonallack, but couldn't quite match his vastly more experienced opponent.

Practising hard and trying to copy the good players that I had watched, my golf was improving rapidly. My handicap was dropping and people at Moortown were beginning to notice me.

That summer I again worked on the course at Alwoodley and went for a couple of lessons with Alf Sanders, Pro at Moor Allerton, paid for by the county. He was surprised how far I could hit it. After I had lost several of his practice balls over the back of the green I was playing to, he suggested I should not hit so hard with the right hand! Alf was also helping another promising Leeds boy at the time, Howard Clark. Howard went on to play in the 1973 Walker Cup and, after turning professional, made six appearances in the Ryder Cup as well as winning eleven European Tour events.

I can't match that record, but if you'd have asked me in 1969 what was to come I would have been full of optimism – particularly on the 8th of April. It was on that day on the the 168 yard 12th at Moortown that I pulled a six iron out of my bag and hit my first hole-in-one! It's a feat that couldn't be achieved today, as the hole no longer exists due to course alterations.

Playing in all possible competitions, I got down to six handicap by mid May. I entered the Yorkshire Amateur Championship at Pannal, and made a great start with a birdie on the first, reaching two under par after five holes, but finished in 76. A second round 83 saw me fail to qualify for the match-play stage.

This intensive spell of golf unfortunately clashed with my O-level exams, and although I got reasonable results, I should have done much better. I won the June medal with a gross 73, hitting 15 greens and taking 36 putts. I then also won the July medal with a 72, making nine straight pars on the back nine, reducing my handicap to three. I had come down from 10 to three in just a year, and won Moortown's Aggregrate Trophy for 1969.

It was a shame that I could not consolidate my position as an up and coming junior star at Moortown, but my Dad had got himself into yet another financial crisis, and the family was on the move again, this time to Lytham St. Annes. The idea was that my grandma, father's mum, would sell her house in Leeds and share a home with us in St. Annes, a place she had always liked. We moved in August, just a couple of weeks after Tony Jacklin had won The Open at Royal Lytham and the place was still buzzing with golf fever. Watching Jacklin triumph in such great style on television inspired me to play in The Open one day...and even win it!

In hindsight, I was bright and should have continued my education with A-levels and university, developing my amateur career as I went. But I was under pressure to earn some money and a job was found for me at a bank in Blackpool.

In the meantime, I had played Fairhaven Golf Club a few times and decided to join as a junior member. Bill Miller, an affable Scotsman and good player who just six years earlier had been Scottish Professional champion, was Pro and Graham Cant was his Scottish assistant. The day before I was due to start at the bank, Bill offered me the position as his second assistant. My Dad and I met Bill that evening for a sort of interview at the old St. Annes Hotel, we agreed terms of £5 per week and I started next day, giving my apologies to the bank!

I didn't realise it at the time, but this was a pivotal moment in my life. On that day in August 1969, under the R&A rules, Britain had a new 16-year-old professional on its books – David Thorp.

But it wasn't the dream introduction to pro-golf I had imagined. My brief amateur career was over, and after playing non-stop competitive golf for the last six months, I would not play another competition round for 10 months. My formal education had also abruptly ended, when there was still so much to learn and such a wide range of careers available to me.

Of course, I couldn't see this at the time. I just wanted to emulate Tony Jacklin and win The Open, becoming a sporting superstar. At Fairhaven, I was stuck for long hours in an old-fashioned pro-shop serving customers, repairing clubs and having to clean endless sets of members' clubs before I could go home each night. Instead of being feted as an up and coming young amateur, winning competitions and rapidly reducing his handicap, I was reduced to the back-room apprentice who only played in the twilight after the shop closed. The members were friendly, but this didn't seem like professional golf to me!

In September I went to Royal Birkdale to watch my first of many Ryder Cups. This was the famous tie when Nicklaus conceded a four foot putt to Jacklin on the final green. A more memorable incident for me was chatting to Lee Trevino on the practice ground. He was the Mexican who had come from nowhere the previous year to win the US Open and was happy to tell me all about the revolutionary solid Faultless ball that he was playing.

It wasn't all bad being the junior assistant at Fairhaven. I joined the PGA in an ongoing association that has now lasted nearly 40 years. The Fairhaven members soon recognised my talent and often invited me to play. Bill was a good teacher and helped my game probably more than anyone else. I wasn't a good bunker player when I arrived, but hard practice in the excellent seaside sand made it one of my strong points. The local assistants such as John Wraith, Geoff Tickell and Graham Cant were keen players and we often used to get a few holes together when work permitted.

We had some great courses in the area including Royal Lytham where I regularly played on my day off, believing that one day I would play there in The Open. My brother Andrew, 10 years my junior was taking an interest in golf and I soon had him hitting balls. A new decade was about to begin – and I was ready to move up a gear.

02

Round The World To Bridgnorth

1970-AGE 16

As I turned 17 in March, my knowledge of golf was really starting to grow. I was learning a great deal through reading, professional help from Bill, exhaustive practice and mixing with other good players. However, competitively, I was stagnating. I was determined to change this. In May, I entered the Graham Textiles tournament at Sandmoor in my home-town of Leeds, and arranged to travel over with John Wraith.

Arrangements with John rarely went smoothly and predictably his car broke down somewhere on the Pennines. Somehow we got there only to find that, due to a mix-up, we were booked into the hotel's honeymoon suite! I spent two uncomfortable nights sharing a bed with John, and had to endure some funny looks at breakfast. This was my first outing as a pro and my first PGA event, and although I hit the ball well, a 78 saw me miss the cut by three shots.

I had to wait a month for my next opportunity, the PGA under-23's championship at St. Annes Old Links, where I had played the British Boys two years earlier. I played poorly for 79, 81, but I did manage the last nine holes in 35, finishing with an eagle three. I missed the cut, but was asked if I would mark for Nick Job in the last round, which I did. As Nick was one of the top young English golfers, I was most encouraged to find that my ball striking was just as good as his.

Shortly afterwards, I played in the PGA Coca-Cola under-25's at Morecambe and Heysham, scoring 80, 70 to miss the cut by five. The second round of 70 at Morecambe was my best yet, but it couldn't make up for the poor first round. Three tournaments played and not a penny won, I was a failure in my mind, but in reality, it was a big step from the medals at Moortown to professional events and I had done OK. A milestone was then passed, I broke 70 for the first time, a five under par 69 at Fairhaven while playing with three members. Having done it once, I was to do it many times in the future.

Suddenly, in August, I found myself moving across the Atlantic once again. I went with my family to Chicago, where my Dad had somehow got a job with the auditing section of the Blue Cross Medical Insurance Company. This was a huge wrench, but Chicago was a bit like Montreal, so it wasn't totally alien and was very exciting. It was however, very hot in August. Needless to say that didn't deter me from playing! There followed another big gap in my competitive career, but a massive amount of golf knowledge and experience was to be gained here.

Through connections with my father's work, I was taken to North Shore Country Club in Glenview. I was introduced to Head Pro Bill Ogden - a big, friendly man and good player. He had a signed photo of Arnold Palmer on his office wall with the inscription " To Bill, a great guy", I was well impressed! North Shore was a high-class, old-money type of place, which had hosted the 1933 US Open, won by Johnny Goodman, the last amateur to win that famous title. It was a fine tree-lined course in lovely condition. I was amazed by the watered fairways which made your drive stop very quickly. They were better than many greens I had encountered in the past.

They were most welcoming to me at North Shore, and after I had played several times with Bill and his assistants, they created a part-time job as "starter" specifically for me. I couldn't get enough of playing on such a superbly manicured course and was relishing it. I was having some trouble hooking, and had a lesson from assistant Bob Lueke, who, very strangely it seemed to me, was in his fifties. Bob told me to weaken my right hand grip, and that seemed to do the trick.

A pro called Jack Bell spent a lot of time at North Shore whilst between club jobs, but not just ordinary jobs. He had just left Medinah in Chicago and was about to start as head Pro at La Jolla Country Club in San Diego. We played and practised together, and he taught me a great practice game on fast greens, 'nearest to the hole', useful for getting the pace of putts. Jack gave me a pair of red and white (!) Foot-joy shoes and was very kind. The Titleist rep called one day and gave me a dozen balls. I couldn't believe the generosity.

After a few weeks, I was offered a position as assistant to Bill Ventresca, a former assistant to Bill Ogden, at Rolling Green Country Club in Arlington Heights. This was not quite as up-market as North Shore, but was a smart facility, reputedly popular with the infamous Chicago mafia in the past. Everyone was so welcoming, as Americans generally are, and I got on well with fellow-assistants Bud Poremba and Ron Schofield.

Bill helped me with my game and I improved well. I had a couple of away-days with other local assistants to good courses. One was to Big-Foot Country Club in Wisconsin and the other to Cog-Hill in Chicago where we played the famous Dubsdread number four course, current venue of the PGA Tour's Western Open. The ninth was 620 yards, easily making it the longest hole I had ever played.

Fellow assistant Ron bet me that I wouldn't break 80 at Cog Hill. Playing off the back tees in searing heat I shot 80 to narrowly lose the bet. I also played at three local munis, Wilmette, Glenview Park and Sportsman.

One day I took my brother Andrew, aged seven, to play on a course for the first time at Rolling Green. Most of my playing took place on Mondays, because on that day all the clubs used to close for maintenance, and only the staff were allowed to play.

Things were great at Rolling Green, I was making $100 a week, which seemed like a fortune to me. One day an old weather-beaten man came into our shop. He was introduced to me as local legend

Rolling Green Country Club, Chicago, USA, 1970.

Johnny Revolta, PGA champion in 1935 and a top player in those days. I think he went out for a game with some members.

Due to the windy city's harsh winters, the courses close around November and re-open in the spring. Bill offered to continue to employ me as assistant from April 1971, which was great. But I had more immediate concerns with no work for several months. It was then that Jack Bell asked me to go and help him at La Jolla over the winter. This sounded great, but being only 17 years old, going to California by myself was a bit scary!

There were, however, other problems emerging. It became apparent that my visa didn't allow me to continue working in the US, and it was unclear how to renew it. My father seemed to be in another crisis, both financially and mentally. He had lost his job and the atmosphere at home was tense. My parents decided to return to England, so that meant my leaving too. It must have been tough for my seven-year old brother Andrew, having just got used to American school life. We phoned Bill Miller at Fairhaven, and he kindly agreed to take me back again as assistant, just four months after I had left. It had been a short stay in Chicago, immensely valuable to me from a golf point of view, but very disappointing, I am sure, for the rest of the family.

In December 1970 the Thorp family flew into a dark, damp and dismal Heathrow airport, repatriated by the British government. My father had problems to sort out with the authorities and I was found digs near Fairhaven Golf Club. This was a time of strikes, power cuts and Britain in crisis under the new Prime Minister Edward Heath. I was now on £8 per week after making the equivalent of £40 a week in Chicago. It got dark early and it was miserable. I couldn't wait for more tournament opportunities.

I had a new set of Titleist clubs, an old Power-Bilt putter that I found in the basement of Bill Ogden's shop and lots of memories, but my American adventure was over. I had learned an incredible amount in four months in The States and undoubtedly returned to England a better player.

1971-AGE 17

Although my family was in disarray, moving from place to place, I was quite happy, single-minded and determined to be a successful tournament player. Mother, Father, Andrew and myself eventually moved into 50 Park Road, St.Annes, which they ran as holiday flats with Grandma living downstairs at the front.

I played a couple of alliances in the New Year, without success, then played in the Alliance Championship at Clitheroe, scoring a respectable 78, 75, but finishing out of the prizes. Soon after I went down to South Herts to try and qualify for the Daks Tournament. This was the big league, and I was so naïve and inexperienced.

I went down to London on the train with my big golf bag and suitcase, then caught the underground to Totteridge. What an adventure! They were very kind at South Herts and one of the members put me up near the course. While having a practice round I saw the great Bobby Locke playing. He looked the antithesis of a big star to me - a rather portly, elderly man with plus-fours and a white cap, hitting everything with a big draw. I met Dai Rees, the Pro, and saw the sculpture in the clubhouse of Harry Vardon's hands, demonstrating his famous overlapping grip which many (including myself) have copied. Vardon had been Pro at South Herts before Rees and was the superstar of his day. I played very well in the qualifying, hitting 15 greens and scoring 75, missing out by just two shots, an excellent effort.

I was understandably keen to play again, but I would have to wait another seven weeks for my next opportunity due to things getting busy at Fairhaven.

It was then that my long fascination with The Open began with a visit to the 1971 event at Royal Birkdale. This was the first of Lee Trevino's two consecutive victories, where he was chased by Mr. Lu in his "pork-pie" hat. One of our members, Geoff Birtwell, a talented, unorthodox player had qualified, so I watched him and was completely knocked out by the atmosphere. Being able to get so close to the great players of the day was fantastic. I was amazed as I watched Nicklaus, Palmer, Trevino and others, and dreamed of one day playing against them.

*Graham Cant (with hose) and Bill Miller at
Fairhaven Pro Shop, Lancashire, 1971.*

My next tournament was the PGA under-23's at Royal Lytham, right on my doorstep. Disappointingly, I missed the cut with 79, 81. A creditable 77 in a Pro-am at the challenging Hillside G.C. was followed by an attempt to qualify for the Benson and Hedges tournament at Fulford. I was on Strensall, scoring 75, and missed by four.

I thought I was failing, not yet having won a penny, but I had jumped in at the deep end, trying to compete with players much older and more experienced than myself. Looking back, this was a mistake, but it was thrilling and every round felt like my big break. Finally, I made a breakthrough.

Playing in the Northern PGA Championship at Moortown, my former club, with my old school-mate John Ingham on the bag, I shot 75, 74 to finish 15th in a field of 127, nine behind winner Lionel Platts. The £5 I won was my first prize money as a professional. I had arrived!

Or had I? My final tournament of the year was the Northern PGA under-25's at West Lancs, but I failed to feature.

Bill seemed sympathetic to my ambitions, and allowed me to play in the Fylde Alliances over the winter of '71-'72. This was a good decision, and with excellent support from the Fairhaven members, I set about the alliances with methodical precision. I had now passed my driving test, so I was able to travel more easily in my own car.

In November I spent two weeks at the Lilleshall Sports Centre on the PGA Assistants' training course. Proudly driving down to Shropshire in my newly acquired grey Wolsley 1500, it soon became apparent that my £100 vehicle had not been a wise investment. Following a puncture, I jacked it up only to find the jack slowly appearing inside the car, as the rusty floor gave way! It got me home again, but I then had to persuade the bank manager to lend me £300 to buy a better set of wheels - a natty turquoise and white Riley Kestrel - which was to prove much more reliable.

Lilleshall was a valuable learning experience, with tutor Doug Smith being particularly helpful with my swing. I passed with an excellent report and would become a full PGA member in 1972.

UNIROYAL
NORTHERN PGA CHAMPIONSHIP
1971

Sponsored by

£1,000 – 36 HOLES STROKE PLAY

MOORTOWN GOLF CLUB, LEEDS
(by kind permission of the Club)

THURSDAY 26th AUGUST	FRIDAY 27th AUGUST
18 Holes	18 Holes

Official Programme   **Admission Free**

Scene of my first professional pay day.

1972–AGED 18

In January I had the first of several lessons from the great John Jacobs at a driving range that he owned in Blackpool. He used to give free tips to local assistants if they were keen enough to come. I remember his first comments were "Good clubhead path. Put right hand more on top and hold on tight. Clear left hip quicker." I was getting stronger and my all-round game was improving. My bunker shots, which had been a weakness, had now become a strength through lots of practice in the perfect Fairhaven sand.

I had terrific success in the alliances, finishing first Pro no fewer than seven times, amassing £111 in winnings over the winter season. I broke par on a number of occasions and was under 70 three times, the best of which was a three under par 69 at St. Annes Old Links. My Alliance stroke average was 73.1.

My winning ways in the alliances attracted the attention of the local press when the Blackpool Evening Gazette published an article about me in early '72. Quotes included "He is a strong boy with good potential and quite a useful performer" from Eddie Musty, Pro at Royal Lytham, and from Bill Miller, my boss at Fairhaven "He must be as good as anybody of his age". Enough to get any 18-year-old thinking of the bigtime.

In April I failed by four shots to pre-qualify for another Tour event, the Piccadilly Medal, at Southport and Ainsdale with a 79, but finished with an encouraging back nine of 36. I still thought I was failing, but tournaments like this were still way out of my league.

Bill must have been very accommodating, because just the following week I was off again, this time to the Leeds Cup, a prestigious Northern PGA tournament, at Carlisle Golf Club. I liked the course, and in the pre-tournament Pro-am shot a one under par 70, finishing fifth out of 47 pros. Unfortunately, there was no prize.

In the main event, paired with good left-hander Mike Nutter in cold and windy conditions I had eight birdies over the two rounds, scoring 76, 74 to finish 30th out of 120 pros, a good performance for me but not good enough to win anything.

After three weeks back at the club, I was off again to the Coca-Cola under-25's PGA championship at Bristol and Clifton and Long Ashton golf clubs in Bristol. This was a great adventure - my third attempt in this event, a few days away in a big city, playing with others of a similar age with my form steadily improving.

From a massive field of 308, the numbers were cut drastically to just the leading 40 for the last two rounds at Long Ashton. After a wobbly first 27 holes, I played the back nine at Long Ashton in 34, to get through on the mark at 149. I then shot two rounds of 72 to finish 17th on 293, 15 shots behind winner Peter Oosterhuis. I was delighted. Not only was this my first completed 72 holes, but I had won £62.40! I was so inexperienced I rang Bill to ask him how I get the money. He said " Come home, they will send it to you"!

The Fairhaven members then kindly sponsored me to play in the 1972 Open at Muirfield. For the qualifying I was drawn at Gullane no.2, a superb, but not too difficult Scottish links. I stayed at Bissets Hotel in Gullane, and played three practice rounds, soaking up the atmosphere. I played reasonably well in qualifying, only getting into my stride in the last nine holes, scoring 76, 72 to miss out by eight shots. It was then that I realised these guys were seriously good! My partners were John Bland and David Russell, both of whom would subsequently become leading players.

A little deflated, but keener than ever to prove myself, I then played in the inaugural Lancashire PGA under-23's championship at Stand Golf Club. I had decided to play with a fade, and this was working well. Paired with Denis Durnian, in the first round I was one under par with three to play, when I suddenly had two shanks, unusual for me, and finished in 75.

I spent the lunch-break on the practice ground, deciding that I had got a bit flat, and came out ready for action in the second round. I played some great stuff, getting to five under after 12 holes, having three times holed out from off the green. Arriving at the last tee with a seven shot lead, I didn't manage to finish in style, hitting my second shot from a bunker out of bounds through the back of the green to make a double bogey six. However, it didn't matter, I still won by five and my 69 was a new course record. My reward was £50 in cash and a sparkling trophy!

Again I was swinging too flat, but with some help from Bill and some hard practice, things were improving. My new key was to swing upright and turn hips through the ball, very much like Jack Nicklaus. It didn't quite work in the Northern PGA under-25's at Southport and Ainsdale, but I knew it would sooner or later.

I also worked hard on my putting with Bill, who was a fantastic putter until the yips got him. He was a great believer in getting a perfect strike to achieve maximum roll on the ball. He liked to see a putt that looked as if it would be short but rolled and rolled until it just went in or crept past the hole.

It was very busy at Fairhaven during the holiday period, which inconveniently interfered with my golf, but when September came I found myself in a select field of 16 young professionals for the Lord Derby's PGA under-25's match-play at Royal Birkdale.

This was to be my first experience of playing the great course, where I had watched the Open and Ryder Cup in previous years. I was drawn against John McTear, a diminutive Scotsman who was to be in my PGA Cup team some years later. The first round was played in perfect conditions and I hit the ball superbly, culminating in three consecutive perfect long irons into the 12th, 13th and 14th greens to win the match five and four.

I was playing well and confidently going into the last eight when fate conspired to put me out in the next round. The day was cold, wet and windy which put my caddy off and he failed to turn up. Nobody else was available and I just couldn't cope with the conditions. Peter Cowen easily beat me seven and six, and I came away with £50.

I entered one more big tournament in 1972: the Wills Open in Edinburgh. Pre-qualifying was at Ratho Park, where ground conditions were firm. Although I played well for 73, I missed out by one shot. Unlucky again, but the closest yet to getting into a Tour event.

The '72-'73 alliance season began and I had a hiccup in form, finishing out of the prizes in the first six events. By this time Graham Cant had left Fairhaven to take up the Pro's position at Colville Park in his native Scotland. His replacement was local boy and friend of mine John Wraith, who had previously worked for John Jacobs at Blackpool Driving Range.

Mixing with other young players around the country, I had heard of the African Safari Tour, taking place in the early New Year in various exotic locations. I rather fancied going and it had to be better than the cold, damp English winter. I got details and an elderly Fairhaven member, Mrs. Hardy, kindly gave me £100 towards the cost. With Bill's blessing I booked my place for Nigeria in February. I couldn't wait!

Funds were a bit tight towards Christmas, since my usual alliance winnings had dried up, but it had been a year of progress. My 1972 stroke average was 75.2 and I had won £242. I was the Lancashire Assistant's champion at 19, only six years after starting to play golf. Next year looked promising.

1973-AGED 19

The New Year started well. My alliance form had returned and the small but regular prize-money was coming my way again. Just prior to the African trip, I swept the board in the singles alliance at St. Annes Old Links with a superb two-under par 38 points to win the maximum £18!

In February I set out on the first of what would be six African Safari Tours. Arriving in Lagos was a severe culture shock. It was so hot, sweaty, dirty and dangerous, but just like everywhere we went in Africa, the hosts were wonderfully accommodating, putting us up free of charge.

Ikoyi golf course was like no other I had ever experienced - dead flat on tree lined scrubland with no proper grass to speak of, making for poor sandy lies. The greens were browns (sand covered in oil) each with its own sweeper-man to keep it smooth.

My first round was in a huge Pro-am, where each pro in the field of 100 was partnered by one amateur. Out in the morning, I played well to score one under par 70, and with the help of my partner Victor Ologundudu - a jovial Nigerian high-handicapper - we had a better-ball 62. This was in the company of Tommy Horton - by far the best player I had played with to date - and his partner. It was a long hot day and Victor spent several hours in the bar celebrating our score...

By early evening there were five teams on 62 and it was decided we would have a sudden-death play-off. Poor Victor was in no state to play any more holes, but he managed to get to the tee. The first three pairs played the first, a par-five, and waited by the brown. When it was our turn, Victor hit one into the left trees and was not seen again, so it was up to me. I hit a good drive followed by a superb three wood just off the back of the brown, then putted into the hole for an eagle three to win the play-off. Prize money of £130 was my biggest win yet. Victor was ecstatic and insisted on taking me to his home that evening to introduce me to his family! My Pro-am victory got national press coverage back home and was a great start to the tour.

After the excitement of the Pro-am, the Nigerian Open got underway. I was brought down to earth with a bump. Although I had four birdies, my first round of 77 left a lot to do. Playing really well in the second round for 71 I just made the cut, but was having real trouble hitting off the sandy lies. I it nine heavy shots over the two rounds. It got to 50 degrees centigrade in the middle of the day, but I did well, shooting 72, 71 in the last two rounds to finish 43rd, just out of the money.

On to Nairobi, which was quite a nice place back in 1973, the suburbs very much like a tropical England might be after global warming! We played at Muthaiga Golf Club, a pleasant parkland course with very nappy greens and red soil, with an old colonial-style clubhouse. Clubbing became very tricky, since the high altitude of Nairobi combined with the intense heat made the ball fly for miles. The grainy greens were also puzzling, and although I hit the ball well, I had too many putts scoring 303 to finish 41st.

During a practice round at Muthaiga, I experienced a very rare bird on the par-five 10th hole - an albatross! Playing in a four-ball with three other Pros, I had hit a poor drive down the left side and proceeded to hit a nice four wood shot that rolled into the hole for a two! Shame it wasn't in the tournament.

Finally, the group headed to Zambia for three weeks. In contrast to Nigeria and Kenya it was very lush, the courses played long and the greens were slow. First we played Ndola, an industrial town where the ex-pats worked hard and played hard: a bit of a shock to a young lad like me. If you could stay sober the course was interesting to play, with its large termite mounds defining the holes. I performed steadily all week, scoring mid-seventies every round, but again not quite good enough for a prize.

Mufulira, a famous copper mining area, was our next location. Like Ndola, it was a long par 73 course with big ant-hills and grainy greens. After the warm-up Pro-am I started the tournament well with a 73, putting me in 16th position, but followed with 80, 75, 75 to finish 44th. Once again, just out of the money. I had played the first two rounds with Irishman Eamon D'Arcy. I was amazed at his unorthodox swing, but he was to go on to great things, including four Ryder Cup appearances.

I knew I was playing well and was determined to make an impact in the final event, the Zambia Open in the capital city, Lusaka. Things started to happen for me in the Pro-am, after birdieing the first two holes I finished birdie, eagle, but still only scored 76.

I played the first 36 holes again in illustrious Irish company, Jimmy Martin, who had made one Ryder Cup appearance in 1965 and Christy O'Connor JR, who was destined for Ryder Cup stardom in the future. I began well, one under after four holes, then a bad patch put me five over after 10, but a storming finish including an eagle on 14 and birdie on 18 saw me round in 75.

A great ball striking second round (17 greens in regulation) gave me a 73, 23rd position. A solid third round of 73 including four birdies put me 21st going into the final round. This was better. The last round, paired with Paul Herbert and Jan Dorrestein, both good players, started badly, par, bogey, bogey. But then I really got going with six birdies in the last 14 holes, including three two-putt birdies on the par-five's, I scored a one under par 72.

My one over par total of 293 put me in 16th place, 12 behind winner Craig Defoy, and won nearly £150. I was delighted. I had learned so much in my five weeks in Africa playing in such varied conditions and had got to know most of the touring professionals. Furthermore, I had made a small profit.

Soon after returning home, it was the Fylde Alliance Championship at St. Annes Old Links, scene of previous successes. It seemed incredibly cold, after six weeks in the tropics but I really fancied my chances. Playing with Geoff Birtwell, I started well and shot 71 to be in the lead. A mediocre second round of 76, including a birdie, birdie finish was still good enough to finish top Pro, but Birtwell beat me by three shots to take the title. I won £133 and was full of confidence.

Then something happened which could have helped but did, in fact, hinder my career. A Blackpool night-club owner and entrepreneur, Paddy McGinty offered to sponsor me. Paddy had previously been in boxing and had reputedly trained leading fighter Brian London. He was to give me a car, get me fit, pay my expenses and take half my winnings. It lasted about four weeks when he decided, for no apparent reason, that he was withdrawing from the agreement. There was some consultation with solicitors and the inevitable publicity in the press, but the sponsorship was over and I would carry on as before.

The sponsorship fiasco and an unfortunate collision between my maroon Triumph Toledo and a lamp-post had upset me a little and my form had suffered as a result. One valuable experience happened in this period, however. I played with Alex Caygill in the Leeds Cup at Pontefract, and marked his card as he won the tournament. Alex was an interesting golfer with a swashbuckling style and a wicked temper. He had been a Ryder Cup player in the 1969 match at Birkdale and was helpful to me. As we played together, I carelessly hit one out of bounds and Alex really laid into me with "All that ----ing golf course on the right and you hit it OB left!" It was a comment I have never forgotten.

My little brother Andrew was now a keen player and at 10 years old already had a 20 handicap at Fairhaven. I had developed my teaching style with Andrew and it was great to see my advice helping his game.

Soon I was back on form and had a major breakthrough, after six failures I qualified for a European Tour event, the Benson and Hedges match-play at Hillside. I got through at Southport and Ainsdale with a 73, including some accurate driving, hitting 13 out of 14 fairways, and birdied the last to get into a play-off, in which I scraped through. I was drawn against Jose-Maria Canizares, an up and coming Spaniard who was destined for great things in the future. Playing in front of a sizeable gallery, neither of us played well on the front nine, and with six holes changing hands, we turned all-square. He then showed his class with three straight birdies and two pars and suddenly I had lost five and four. My consolation was a £20 cheque. It had been exciting to play in my first tour event as a 19 year-old, only four years after being just an up and coming junior at Moortown.

I then made an ill-advised trip to the French Open in Paris. Driving over in my car with Ian Bolt, another young pro, we miscalculated how long the journey would take and after many hours of travel, arrived in the middle of a wet Parisian night, with nowhere to stay. It seemed to rain constantly and the whole week was a costly disaster. You learn from experiences like this!

After a disappointing first round exit in the Lancs PGA matchplay at Clitheroe courtesy of Colin Smith, it was off to the Coca-Cola under-25's at Bristol, the tournament I had done well in last year. Partnering star Australian Bob Shearer was a good experience but an opening 79 put me well off the pace. In the second round, matching Shearer shot for shot, I shot a fine 69 at Bristol and Clifton but missed the cut by a single stroke.

That round was the start of a good run of form. In the Lancs PGA Championship at Fulwood, Preston, a course I was unfamiliar with, I played some excellent stuff to be four under par with two rounds of 70 to finish second to Jimmy Hulme and won £60.

A few days later I was defending my Lancs PGA under-23's title at Haydock Park, and after my good result at Fulwood I was very much the favourite. An eventful tournament started with a bogey, then four birdies in the next 11 holes got me to three under. A lost ball on the 13th and two further birdies and I was round in a three under par 67. I had ten threes in the round and was in the lead. One under after eight in the second round and I seemed to be cruising, but then a series of mishaps got me to the point where I had to hole a 15 foot putt on the last for a 76 to get into a play-off. Fortunately, I managed this and tied with Denis Durnian and my fellow Fairhaven assistant John Wraith.

In the sudden-death we all parred the first two holes, although mine were both scrambled up and downs. On the third, a par five, Denis eliminated himself by going OB, I was in trouble and made six and John was left needing just two putts for a winning par from ten feet. He three-putted so we were off again. The fourth was halved in par threes, with John again missing a great chance from eight feet. On the par five fifth we were both just short in two. John thinned his pitch over the green into thick rough. Then in dramatic style I played a perfect sand-wedge from 40 yards into the hole! I had retained the trophy and collected £41.

Even though we must have split the prize-money John didn't speak to me for a while, but that tournament taught me that there is more than one way to put a score together - and that it's OK to win ugly.

Next it was my second attempt to qualify for The Open. This was to be Tom Weiskopf's solitary major victory at Troon. I was drawn at Glasgow Gailes and in a practice round I teamed up with American amateur Danny Edwards, who was to go on to be successful on the PGA Tour. He would be leading amateur in this Open and then go on to win all four of his matches in the 1973 Walker Cup. I did not play too well in the qualifying, scoring 152 to miss out by seven shots.

In a Pro-am at the very testing links of Hillside I had a superb ball striking round, hitting 15 greens in regulation, but took 38 putts for a 75. Shortly after this it was the Northern PGA under-25's at Worsley. Conditions were atrocious, heavy rain all day, never good for me. However, I battled through determinedly to finish 12th with rounds of 74 and 79.

Following another unsuccessful attempt to qualify for the B and H at Strensall there was a new tournament, the Lancashire Open, at my favourite venue St. Annes Old Links. After recently finishing runner-up in the Lancashire Pro's Championship and winning the Lancashire PGA under-23's Championship, I was really up for this one. Paired with Ian Gradwell and Bob Rogers in dry and windy conditions, I hit the ball well in round one but struggled with the putter to score a disappointing 79. The afternoon round started on a much more promising note when, after a perfect drive down the first, my wedge shot finished three inches from the hole. With improved putting I compiled a 70, the best second round of the day, to finish 12th, eight behind winner Alex Caygill. My reward was £40.

The Northern PGA championship was at West Lancs, a course I always found difficult, and although I played steadily, 77, 75 was not good enough for a prize.

In September 1973 I went up to the Muirfield Ryder Cup in Scotland with local Blackpool Park assistant Robert McAndrew. We had a great time watching Nicklaus, Palmer, Weiskopf, Trevino, Jacklin, Oosterhuis and many more. We also managed to fit in 36 holes at Gleneagles and a round at Carnoustie. Quite a trip!

The main competitive season was over and I felt I had done pretty well, but my own campaign continued with the new alliance season beginning. We started, strangely enough, with the main event: the 36 hole Fylde Alliance Championship at Blackpool North Shore. I had finished runner-up in last season's championship, which, since it took place at the end of the season, had been just six months earlier. On a dry, windy day I had a fantastic spell with the putter in round one, using it only 26 times for a one under par 71. I continued to play solidly in the afternoon, but the putter cooled down resulting in a 73, which tied me for first place with Preston Professional Jim Gove. Going out in a sudden-death play-off we halved the first two holes in disappointing bogeys, then Jim birdied the third to beat me. Another good result, however, bringing me more winnings.

There followed a singles alliance at my home club, Fairhaven, which attracted national publicity for the remarkable finish to my round. I was hitting it great but couldn't hole a thing for 13 holes and was one over par with five to play. I then made four straight birdies and finished off with an eagle three on the 18th. I had made consecutive putts of 20, 15, four, 15 and 15 feet on the last five holes. This was probably my best ball striking round to date, hitting 17 of 18 greens in regulation, including a par five in two, and getting inside 15 feet on 11 of those 17 occasions. My five under par round of 69 won the competition by three shots and netted me the grand total of £18!

I had a number of other good alliance rounds including a seven-birdie 67 at Ashton and Lea. I also won the inaugural Fylde Assistants Winter League for 1973-74.

All in all 1973 had been a year of great progress. In 62 competitive rounds a stroke average of 74.4 had helped me to win over £750. I was a big strong lad coming up to 21, six feet tall, thirteen and a half stones, a long and straight hitter, good chipper and putter. I had now experienced a lot of tournament play and was keen to reach the top.

My financial position was, however, precarious. My family was not well off, with all my father's money-making schemes seeming to fail, and I had no cash reserves, always relying on the next prize money to supplement my meagre earnings as assistant at Fairhaven. Bill had been very supportive, allowing me lots of unpaid leave to chase my dream, as had equipment manufacturers Penfold and John Letters, who had kept me supplied with balls and clubs. If I was going to carry on playing, I would have to start to make it pay.

1974-AGE 20

This was to be an eventful, but in many ways negative year for my golf. After such a good 1973 I had to go to Africa again, and in January all the arrangements were made. Nigeria was off the agenda this year, and the tour would be five weeks long taking in four tournaments in Kenya and Zambia. Looking ahead, I had given my Dad the entry forms for the European Tour events which were scheduled for just after the Safari Tour – a decision that turned out to be a big mistake.

On Sunday February 24th I flew from Manchester to join the party at Heathrow for our flight to Nairobi. Not playing too well and struggling on the nappy greens I missed the cut in the Kenya Open. This was a new and unpleasant experience for me in Africa which I didn't want to repeat.

Moving to Lusaka, it was very wet most of the week and the tournament was reduced to 54 holes. My putting touch returned in the Pro-am, scoring one over par 74 and renewing my confidence for the main event. Two solid opening rounds of 73 put me in eleventh position. For the third and final round I partnered Stuart Brown, a fine up and coming player, and played steadily for 74 to finish in 14th place, winning £126. A good result.

On to Ndola and on March 13th, my 21st birthday, I played in the pre-tournament Pro-am. My ball striking was superb, missing just one fairway and one green to score level par 73. In the tournament, The Cock of The North, I made a great start, holing putts of 25 and 15 feet for opening birdies. Some ups and downs followed, but I finished with a nice birdie three on the tricky 18th to be round in 74. A second round of 75 had me in 23rd position and then a tremendous five under par 68 in round three pushed me up to 12th place. This was an almost flawless round with five birdies and no bogeys which turned out to be the best round of the day and equal lowest of the tournament. In the last round again excellent striking put me inside 15 feet in regulation ten times, but I was unable to convert enough of those birdie chances and finished with 74. My one under par total of 291 gave me 12th place, only seven shots behind winner Malcolm Gregson, and netted me £213. Another fine week, and one of my best performances in Africa.

The final tournament at Muf (Mufulira) was rather an anti-climax for me. Four mid-seventies rounds put me in 50th place and out of the money. I had played well in two out of four African tournaments and returned home with a modest profit

Arriving back at Heathrow on Tuesday March 26th, I somehow managed to play the very next day in an alliance at Blackpool North Shore scoring 72 and winning £5! In my absence, my Dad had not only entered me for the first four European Tour events on the continent, but had also booked me on the same package as the star players including Tony Jacklin, staying in top hotels. I suppose I must have agreed to this, but in retrospect it looks an unwise move. It gave me two main problems. Firstly I had to leave my assistant's job at Fairhaven, although Bill and the club were happy for me to be attached, it would be unpaid. Secondly, I had to pay for this campaign. The Fylde Alliance kindly gave me £100 in sponsorship and I negotiated a loan from my bank, which was enough to get me on tour again.

Less than two weeks after returning from Zambia, I was on my way to Lisbon to play in the Portuguese Open at Estoril, a short, tree-lined course. I was surprised to discover that I had to pre-qualify for all of these events, and with more and more entries on tour, getting through was no formality. My practice round was curtailed by a severe nose-bleed, so I would have to play the course blind. Having recovered in my luxury sea-front hotel, but still wobbly, I got round in 75 and qualified.

I had a great draw for the first two rounds with Jose Canizares and Vicente Fernandez, both already successful players. I played fairly well and comfortably made the cut with 70, 72. The third round was with John Morgan, a steady English player. Starting well and going out in 33 including hitting a seven iron to six inches on the 9th, I was in good shape, but things went badly wrong on the back nine. The tightness of the course and the pressure of having to win money seemed to get to me and a 43 back saw me miss the three round cut by three shots.

A little shell-shocked, I moved on with my illustrious colleagues to La Manga for the Spanish Open. In the qualifying on the North course I started well enough, going out in 36, but developed some swing problems on the back nine to shoot 79 and miss out by six. A bit of a disaster, but at least I had the whole week to practise and could watch some top players. I remember seeing young whizz-kid, Seve Ballesteros in what I believe was his first pro tournament and watched Gary Player play an awesome array of bunker shots.

Next it was the Madrid Open. Apart from struggling with my swing, I had the added problem of being unable to afford to eat properly or get my laundry done due to staying in such an expensive place. Unlike the Safari Tour where we stayed in private homes, on the real circuit everything had to be paid for and my money had all but run out. There was no pre-qualifying, but I played very poorly and was nowhere near the cut.

The final leg of the tour was the French Open at the superb Chantilly course in Paris. I was determined to do well. I just got through the qualifying at The International Club with a 76 and my game was feeling better. In the tournament I played well, but with four three-putt greens in round two, scored 76, 78 to miss the cut by an agonising single shot. I was in crisis now, not even able to afford a meal. Brian Huggett was very kind, buying me dinner and arranging for me to catch an early flight home.

I was entered for the Penfold tournament at Hill Barn in Worthing, but was in no condition to play. I had left my car at the Kingswood home of Bill Gaskell, a wealthy Fairhaven member who worked in London. After the Gaskells had kindly fed me and put me up for the night, I was off to the south coast. I made a good effort in the pre-qualifying, but an eight on the 14th took me to a 77, two shots too many.

On returning to St. Annes on May 7th I discovered I had lost over a stone in weight. I had no job, no cash, my family was poor, I owed the bank money and couldn't afford to enter any more tournaments. I had to stop playing and find a job. Quite a predicament.

I went over to my old home, Leeds, to find employment possibilities. While visiting Moortown for a game, I was chatting to assistant Don Sterling, who told me one of their members was trying to find a Pro to go over to Finland to do some teaching, all expenses paid. It sounded good to me in my current situation, so I rang him. Things moved quickly and before long I was due to sail to Helsinki from Hull on the M.S. Sirius, a container ship on June 5th. I decided to sell my car, my only real asset, in order to pay off my loan, and a local garage obliged.

After a smooth passage lasting three days through the North Sea and the Baltic I arrived in Finland. On the taxi ride to Helsinki Golf Club I was surprised to see how yellow all the grass was and was told things hadn't started to grow yet as their Spring was just beginning, in June! My accommodation in the greenkeeper's house at the club was somewhat basic and not altogether spotless, but it was free. The clubhouse was an old wooden building, but food was provided and this was also most welcome. The Head Pro was a friendly old Finnish man called Sigge Nystrom who was so busy with lessons that another Pro was needed to share the load.

Helsinki was a very cosmopolitan city being the capital of Finland and the golf club attracted a wide range of nationalities. Fortunately, English was a common language but communication was sometimes difficult, which forced me to learn how to speak clearly in order to make my lessons understood. I was kept busy and didn't get much time to play. I did, however practise a lot and it was handy having the chipping green outside my bedroom window!

The course was nothing special, but as you might expect in Finland, there was no shortage of trees and with a number of rocky outcrops, it was interesting to play. The driving range was open-air, offering no shade from the fierce summer sun and we hit off grass. It was incredibly hot and the local mosquitoes were vicious, but everyone was very kind to me.

One big disappointment about being in Finland in July was missing The Open at Royal Lytham. With the qualifying courses so familiar to me, I would have had a great chance of getting through. I saw some of it on television, including Gary Player's left-handed putt from next to the clubhouse while on his way to victory.

My lesson diary was filling up and without many outgoings I was able to save some money. As the job was due to end in the Autumn I started to think about what to do next. I still wanted to play tournaments but thought I needed some reliable income apart from winnings. I couldn't ask Bill to employ me again after messing him about so much and since I was now PGA qualified, the sensible option seemed to be to apply for club professional jobs back in England. My mother sent over Golf Illustrated magazine every week, so I was able to see the up-to-date adverts. I wrote for a number of jobs and asked them to reply to my home address in St. Annes. It would be interesting to see the replies. As a 21-year old I would be very young to be a club pro, so I wasn't hopeful of success.

As August drew to a close in Helsinki, the temperature had dropped and Autumn had already arrived for this northerly city. I was getting pretty fed up with the monotony of constant lessons and had achieved my aim of getting some cash together, so it seemed a good time to go home. With some help from the members I was able to exchange my Finnish marks for pounds sterling and I was booked on the Sirius for the return journey to Hull at 10.00a.m. Saturday 31st August 1974.

Keeping my cash safe on the voyage was my main concern and I managed that, but another problem, keeping my breakfast down, and that was beyond my control! We met force nine gales in the

North Sea and I thought I was going to die in the massive seas, but the crew didn't seem unduly concerned. After a lengthy delay we finally docked at Hull and I was relieved to be back on dry land. My Dad was there to meet me and we drove back to Lytham.

Back in St. Annes I was keen to resume my tournament career and after less than two days back on English soil I was teeing off in the 1974 Lancashire Open at St. Annes Old Links. It seemed like I had never been away, but understandably my game was a little rusty. I was paired for the first time with my old boss Bill Miller, and I was eager to show him how well I could play. In windy, wet conditions I started well with 75 to be lying fifth, but after three-putting the first two greens in round two shot 77 to finish ninth.

Sadly this was to be my last Lancashire event before moving away. The Fylde Alliance and the county and regional tournaments had been a great training ground for me, as well as an important source of income. Everyone involved had been supportive and encouraging and I would always be grateful.

The replies to my job applications were arriving. Perranporth Golf Club in Cornwall wrote to say they were interested in me but maybe it would be a bit dull there in the winter for a 21-year old. Although it now sounds idyllic, at the time I agreed with them and chose not to pursue it. However, two clubs invited me for interview: Bridgnorth in Shropshire and Shortlands in London. I bought myself a cheap Morris 1300 car for £159 and off I went.

Bridgnorth seemed like a nice friendly club in a pleasant Shropshire town. The interview seemed to go well as far as I could tell and then I was off to London for the Shortlands meeting the next day. This was a completely different place, a cramped nine hole course in a built up area. I soon decided it wasn't for me. Soon after returning home to Lancahire, I was invited to bring my clubs for a second interview at Bridgnorth. Being extremely confident in my playing ability at that time, I knew I could impress them and by the end of the day on September 19th the job was mine and I was due to start just over two weeks later.

I never had any real ambition to be a Club Professional. Having seen the poor down-trodden Pros at some clubs, I really didn't want to be like them. I just wanted the backing of a steady business to enable me to pursue my tournament ambitions and since I was PGA qualified this seemed the way to go. Bridgnorth and later Sutton Coldfield were tolerant and mostly encouraging but inevitably there were occasional conflicts of interest.

Suddenly I had other priorities apart from my own golf - I had to fit and stock a shop and find an assistant. Fortunately accommodation was provided in a semi-detached house which the club owned adjacent to the 15th fairway, and a small retainer would be paid. I had about £500 to invest in golf stock, which seems an impossibly small amount these days, but with some extended credit from suppliers I was able to get started. My mother and brother came down to help decorate the shop and sort out the house and Richard Joyce, a young Fairhaven member and former alliance partner joined me as assistant and everything was ready to go!

Bridgnorth was a small but growing golf club in 1974. A nine hole course for many years, it gained a second nine a short time before my arrival. This was made possible by the closure of the railway line by Dr. Beeching in the sixties which made land available to double the size of the course. The clubhouse at that time was an old cricket pavilion with a tin roof and the wooden shop resembled a neglected broom cupboard.

The previous pro was an old gentleman called Willis Evans who used to double up as the greenkeeper. It was nothing like Fairhaven but I was the Pro and the members were supportive of my shop and my playing. The course and practice ground were muddy in the winter, unfamiliar conditions to me, but I practised hard for the year ahead. I gave quite a number of lessons soon after starting and it seems incredible now that my fee at the time was only £1.10 for half an hour.

Richard decided the assistant's life wasn't for him after a few weeks and returned to Lancashire, but in a short time I found a replacement. Andy Arrowsmith joined me as a five handicapper from Walsall Golf Club. He soon became an asset to my business as well as a friend, enabling me to go playing without worrying about the shop. Andy went on to become Pro at Ludlow and Beau Desert and has been a respected teacher in Germany for some years now.

I played in about eight Staffs and Shropshire alliances and winter league events up to the end of 1974 without much success. This was, I think for three reasons. Firstly, I didn't know the courses, secondly, I didn't know any of the other players and thirdly, I wasn't used to playing heavy inland courses.

It had not been a year of progress for my game; I seemed to have been a better player early in the year than at the end. However, I had gone from a dire financial position in May to relative stability in December.

Going on that expensive excursion to Europe for just four tournaments in the Spring had been a big mistake which had undoubtedly caused the remainder of the year to be a write-off from a playing point of view. I was now a club professional with a business to run, but still saw myself primarily as a player.

03

A Rosie Outlook

1975-AGED 21

Over Christmas I had decided to seek the club's permission to go on the African Safari Tour again, which would be my third time. They had no hesitation in agreeing and I started to prepare for the five-week tour which included Nigeria, Kenya and Zambia. Assistant Andy would hold the fort in my absence, with the help of his Dad.

I was feeling confident when we flew out of Heathrow on February 12th on an over-night flight destined for Lagos. I knew what to expect this time so my second visit to Nigeria was not as shocking as the first time. We started with a Pro-am at Ibadan, and after a hair-raising bus journey I played OK for a 74 and won a small cheque. Ikoyi was the main venue and in the warm-up Pro-am I made a great start with three straight birdies, but finished on one over par 72. In the Nigerian Open my first round of 76 left me well down the field. Round two was better and another hat-trick of birdies on the back nine helped me to 71, just making the cut. In the third round, playing with a young Shropshire lad, Tony Minshall, I started fast to be four under after seven holes and finished with 69 to move up to 50t^h place. The fourth round was a bit mixed but a mere 22 putts and yet another triple run of birdies gave me a 70 for a 286 total for 40th place. It had been a gritty fight-back and I had won just under £100.

On to Kenya and another new Pro-am venue, Karen Golf Club, an excellent tree-lined course where lions occasionally wander from the surrounding jungle on to the course! After getting to two under par after five holes my own round petered out to a 77, but my partner and I managed an amazing better-ball 59 to finish in second place, winning me £86. The Kenya Open was again at Muthaiga and although I was hitting it well, I just couldn't work out the greens. Five three-putts in 36 holes helped me to 76, 75, barely making the cut. While in Nairobi I stayed with a larger then life character called John Soborg. John was a Danish jazz musician, a great, laid-back guy who liked to mix with the rich and famous. The night before the third round we had a dinner party and Sean Connery was one of the guests. It was difficult to get much sleep that night! There was now a three round cut and with the third round carrying on much like the others, a 75 gave me an unwelcome day off on Sunday.

Next stop Lusaka. After a 75 in the Pro-am I hit the ball well throughout the tournament but took too many putts. My putting totals were 34, 37, 31 and 33 helping me to a mediocre score of 301. I played the third round with my old Leeds compatriot Howard Clark. I always enjoyed partnering Howard to witness his powerful and crisp striking.

The Mufulira Open followed and after two warm-up pro-ams the main event began. In the first round my ball striking was solid and with average putting I had a two over par 75. Round two, in the company of Nick Job, was a superb performance, my best for a long time. Hitting 12 of 14 fairways, 16 of 18 greens and taking 31 putts resulted in five birdies for a three under par 70 to put me in 15th position. Another good round of 72 on Saturday made me 19th going into day four. After much anticipation it was to be a poor last round of 79 to put me in 38th place with very little prize-money.

Finally it was the big one, the Zambia Open at Ndola, a course I had played well on before. My usual sort of Pro-am score, 75 brought no reward but was a valuable practice round. The par 73 course was playing long and, playing steadily throughout, I scored 75, 73, 73, 74 to finish 20th and won £127. On the day of our departure there was a small Pro-am in the morning organised by the ladies which I managed to win with a two under par 71 to win £50, a nice bonus!

It had been a moderately successful safari. With a stroke average of 74.1 for 27 rounds I had won about £450, enough to make a modest profit thanks to the hospitality of the local hosts.

Back home in Bridgnorth it was a relief to find my shop was still there and that Andy had kept things running well in my absence. There were a few alliances but somehow they didn't excite me like the Fylde Alliance had. For me at that time there was too much emphasis on 'a nice day out' and not enough on the quality of the play. As there were no individual events, winning was very much dependent on the amateur partner and I liked to be in control of my own destiny!

A significant moment happened on April 10th 1975, I met Rosie who was to become my wife a year later. She was a native of Bridgnorth and had just started her career as an Infant Teacher at Chasetown. She didn't play golf but she soon became interested and would caddy for me many times in the future.

My next tournament was the Sumrie Fourball in Bournemouth, on the Meyrick Park and Queens Park courses, in which I partnered my former Fairhaven colleague John Wraith. We got through the qualifying with a 68 and then scored 74, 69, 70 to miss the cut. One round was played with Sam Torrance who was to go on to fame and fortune.

Less than a week later I was off to the south coast again for the Penfold PGA Championship at Royal St. Georges in Sandwich, a venue which would become significant to me in the future but not this week. I was drawn at North Foreland for the pre-qualifying and shared a practice round with David Moore, a very talented English player whose life would be tragically cut short in Zambia a year later. A disappointing 78 failed to get me into the tournament, which Arnold Palmer won in the twilight of his career.

Two rounds of 79 in the Midland Pro's Championship at Peterborough were followed by another 79 in the Ludlow Pro-am. This was poor stuff for me and I didn't understand it. About this

A nice backswing outside my shop, Bridgnorth, Shropshire, 1975.

time something strange started to happen, I would stutter in the middle of my backswing. It was a while before I even noticed it and it didn't seem to affect my shots much, but it did spoil the rhythm of my swing. Little did I know how this little nuisance would develop into something much more sinister in the future.

After a tournament-free week at the club, we had a 36 hole Midland PGA tournament at Redditch, a tricky course with a particularly tough back nine through thick trees. A poor start of 80 put me out of contention but on day two Rosie came to watch me play for the first time and with some extra determination I played a lot better for 75.

Then in 3 consecutive days of play something clicked and I won over £200. I won the first team prize in the Oxley Park Pro-am, then finished second in the Rank-Xerox Pro-am at Edgbaston and followed that with third place in the Midland PGA par-3 championship at Kings Norton. This was encouraging for my next outing to the Open qualifying at St. Andrews New for the main event at Carnoustie. I loved the course but couldn't quite handle it with 77,75 which was, of course, far too many to get through. One good memory of that trip was unofficially playing some holes on the wonderful Old Course late one evening, while I was supposed to be having a practice round on The New!

The Midland Open at Walsall followed and a first round of 71 put me in the mix. A second round 76 dropped me to 18th place, but at least I won a cheque for £25, and things were improving again. A young amateur named Sandy Lyle won this tournament and went on to win a few others!

Rosie came to York with me for another attempt to qualify for the Benson and Hedges at Strensall. I nearly made it with a 74, but would have to wait a while longer before playing in this tournament. The following week was the Second City tournament at Sutton Coldfield. I enjoyed the heathland course and had the privilege of playing with four-time Ryder Cup player Peter Butler but scores of 73, 80 were not good enough to get me into day two. A decent round of 71 in a Pro-am at Penn won me a small cheque and then I was off to attempt to qualify for the PGA match-play at Lindrick. I played well at Worksop and a 74 made me first alternate for the event but nobody dropped out so I didn't get to play.

Another mediocre round of 77 in a Pro-am at Knott End again brought no reward, but then in two county championships, events in which I have always done well, things started to happen. In the Shropshire Open at Oswestry I played some solid golf on an unfamiliar course to score 68, 71 for a one under par 139 to tie for first place with Kevin Bayliss, pro at Ludlow. In the play-off on the par-four first I hit a great drive while my opponent topped his about 100 yards, game over I thought! But golf is a fickle game, Kevin hit a good wood down the fairway and I pushed my 4 iron second shot right of the green. Then he hit a nice wedge to six feet and I had to pitch from a poor lie over a bunker. I played it well but it ran about 15 feet past and then proceeded to miss the putt and tap in for five. Kevin then knocked his in for four to take the title. I had won just over £50 and enhanced my local reputation. The following week I shot 76, 70 at South Staffs to finish fifth in the Staffs and Shropshire Pro Championship which again helped my local standing.

After a few more small pro-ams and alliances my playing year of 1975 was drawing to a close. My play had been generally poor with some exceptions. I had played a lot of golf, over 60 rounds with a stroke average of 74.5 and had won only £750. But I had gone through a lot of changes, new home, new job, steady girlfriend (now fiancee), new courses to play and new opponents to compete against. The small shop business was OK and my teaching had gone well, but with the course and practice ground extremely wet in the winter, lessons and practise activities would be difficult until the spring.

1976-AGED 22

Rosie and I were due to marry in April and perhaps with this in mind I chose not to go to Africa in '76 after going on safari the three previous years. She had conveniently found a teaching post in Bridgnorth to start after the Easter holidays and we would live in the club's house in Stanley Lane.

In February I did, however, go to Portugal to compete in a Pro-am at Vale do Lobo with three Bridgnorth members. I enjoyed the course, a tough par-73 lined with umbrella pines and spectacular sea views of the Atlantic. Fortunately for me the professional field was relatively weak and many of them were more concerned with the eating and drinking than the golf. Playing fairly well I scored 78, 72, 78 to finish second and win £325.

Playing a few alliances, my game was ticking over in readiness for the main season. I jealously kept in touch with the results from the African tour and was shocked to hear about the murder of young professional David Moore in Mufulira. Apparently his host had gone berserk and fatally shot David while Gary Smith, another pro, had narrowly escaped with his life. The man then shot himself dead. These events must have had a devastating effect on the travelling party.

Our wedding went successfully ahead at Morville church near Bridgnorth, with my assistant Andy acting as Best-Man. While on our enjoyable honeymoon in Ibiza, golf was not ignored! We happened to meet a Bridgnorth member, Ken Curwen and his wife on the island, and Ken and I had a game on a pleasant little nine-hole course. Rosie was very understanding!

In early May I played a small Pro's event at the excellent Pleasington Golf Club back in Lancashire and, on a very windy day, shot a 73 to finish second and pick up £120. The following week it was the Piccadilly Medal at Finham Park in Coventry, my first big tournament since the previous summer. The pre-qualifying round was also at Finham and on a dry, windy day I was in top form. Three under par after 16 holes, I was cruising along, but then started to feel ill, a tummy problem. I managed to get my par on the short 17th, but I was in a terrible state going up the last. After an unscheduled pit-stop in the trees on the left I somehow completed the hole in double-bogey six for a 72 which was good enough to qualify! The weather turned cold, windy and wet for the tournament and my rounds of 78, 73 were agonisingly one shot too many for the cut.

A mediocre performance in the Midland Pro's Championship at Longcliffe, scoring 74, 79 was followed by a failed, first attempt to qualify for the Club Professionals Championship at Coxmoor.

Things started to improve again with a nice round of 71 in a small pro-am at Ludlow and by the time I got to the 36-hole Midland PGA tournament at Coventry Hearsall my confidence was high. A good two under par opening round of 68 put me in second spot. I had hit 16 of 18 greens in regulation and had finished the round in great style by holing my second shot on the par 4 18th with a 9 iron. A steady second round of 73 saw me finish in seventh place to win £52.

Next it was another tour event, the Manchester Open, being held at Wilmslow. On a wet and windy day in the qualifying round at North Manchester Golf Club I just did enough to get through with a 75. The Wilmslow course was wet and heavy, which now seems strange since this was the long hot summer of 1976, but the weather was just about to improve, and would stay sweltering until the autumn. In the main event I played well tee-to-green but took too many putts with totals of 34 and 36 for the first two rounds to shoot 77, 73 and miss the cut yet again by a frustrating single shot, exactly the same as in the Piccadilly.

Two weeks later I was off to the Open. In those days the 36 hole qualifying tournament was held on Friday and Saturday and The Open ran from the following Wednesday to a Saturday finish. It was also earlier than it is now, ending on July 10th. I was drawn on Hesketh, a nice links course with which I wasn't familiar although I knew the other Southport courses well. I would be staying at 50 Park Road, my parents' house in St. Annes and it would be nice to see the family again. It was extremely hot and I was drawn with Peter Harrison, who had followed me as Fairhaven Assistant and Andrew (now Chubby) Chandler, who would go on to manage top players such as Lee Westwood and Darren Clarke. The parched course was running so fast that it wasn't easy. I made a good start, going out in 35, one over par, then started back birdie, double-bogey, birdie. Two more birdies, offset by two bogeys had me round in level par 71. I was in fifth place and very much in with a chance. That night and the following morning I was really ill with sunstroke and felt as weak as a kitten! Against all the advice from home I decided I must go for the second round, after all I may never again get such a good chance of qualifying for The Open. I struggled round the front nine in 37 with the help of a few good putts, but a bogey on the 12th put me to three over par, and my chances were slipping away. Then from somewhere I summoned up the strength to make four straight birdies and with pars on 17 and 18 I was round in 71 again to finish in joint second place. Malcolm Gregson was the only player to beat me in the field of 130, and I was in The Open Championship at Royal Birkdale!

My 13 year old brother Andrew, by now an accomplished junior golfer at Fairhaven, was keen to caddy, so with the enthusiastic agreement of his Headmaster to have time off school, his big-time caddying career was about to begin. It was amazing for us both to be rubbing shoulders with star players that we had only seen on TV or watched from the sidelines. We soon discovered that trolleys were not allowed in The Open, unlike the Tour events, so he would have to carry the bag, no mean feat for a youngster.

I hooked up with American Danny Edwards, who I had previously played with and now a rising star on the US Tour, and his fellow countryman Bill Garrett for a practice round. The course was parched and with the greens quite firm and brown in places scoring would be difficult. Practice went well and I couldn't wait for the tournament.

1.50p.m. was my first round starting time, playing with an Italian called Pellegrini and Irishman Jimmy Heggarty. It was a very dry, hot day, so hot in fact that some gorse bushes to the left of the first hole caught fire and had to be extinguished by the fire brigade. The first at Birkdale is a tricky, long par-four that snakes its way between the sandhills and requires an accurate tee-shot. Full of confidence on the first tee, I nailed my 2 iron into the perfect spot and we were away. Hitting my second onto the green I two-putted for an opening par. I played like that all the way round and arrived on the 18th tee one over par. Although it is now a par-four, in 1976 the last at Birkdale was a par-five, and playing as short as it was, a four or even three was possible. I could see from the score-boards that I could well be in the top ten with a good finish. I hit a good straight drive and the green was in range. It was at this moment that (I was told later) the television cameras zoomed in on me and the great Henry Longhurst described my playing of the 18th. After a lengthy wait I hit my 3 wood second shot (which Henry termed an old-fashioned slice!) pin-hi right which wasn't too bad with the flag on the left, but I was a bit close to the spectator fence. I had never played in front of so many people before, but managed to play a nice pitch to about four feet. I made a good stroke at the putt, but had mis-read it and missed. Tapping in for a five, I had shot 73 to be in joint 15th position, ahead of many top players including Jack Nicklaus and was joint leading Englishman. What a dream start! That evening I had many congratulations and Rosie had managed to get permission from school to come round the course with me on Friday for the third round, presuming I was still there!

Andrew and I set out on our second round the focus of much attention. Peter Alliss had picked up on the fact that my 13 year old brother was caddying (courtesy of my Dad, I think) and told the BBC audience what little he knew about me. I was still feeling good, not nervous, but didn't start as well as yesterday. Bogeys on the first, fifth, sixth, eighth, ninth and tenth put me six over after eleven, but the scoring was high and I could still make the cut. Then on the 12th, a great par-three, I found an impossible spot in the front left bunker. It took me three shots to escape and cost me a triple bogey six. A par on the 13th and I was nine over par with five to play. Things were looking bad but five minutes later they looked even worse. My 3 iron to the par-three 14th was pushed into some horrible thick rough on a down-slope with a bunker between me and the pin. All I could do was hack into the bunker. It looked like game over, but then miraculously I hit a perfect bunker shot straight into the hole for a par-three, and played 15 and 16 well, just missing birdies. The last two holes were both reachable par-fives which I took full advantage of to make birdie fours. This roller-coaster ride of a round all added up to 79, just good enough to make the cut. I hadn't played well but I had fought back from a seemingly hopeless position and was now in the remaining 84 players in the world's biggest tournament, wow!

Friday arrived cooler, windy and showery. I had suddenly attracted my own gallery from Bridgnorth and Fairhaven and Rosie had arrived full of encouragement. Andrew was doing a great job, enjoying every minute, there would be plenty to tell his school-friends about on Monday. One of the great things about playing in the Open is that all the golf companies want to give you things. I had cashmere jumpers, shirts, balls, gloves etc. on the understanding that I use them during the tournament. Unfortunately, the one thing that had got me to this point, my golf swing, was not working too well on this morning, but I would try my hardest. I was playing with Scotsman Bill Lockie and we both knew a good score was required if we were to survive the second cut when 84 players would be reduced to 60 and ties for the final round. I started with a nice drive down the first and then shanked my second shot into a wilderness area on the right, never to be seen again, unbelievable! Seven on the first was followed by five on the second and my Open seemed to be over. I battled on to be out in 40, which wasn't that bad as the day's scoring turned out to be high with 11 scores in the 80's, including my 82. I did manage to finish in style with a drive and 2 iron to five feet on the 18th to show my supporters what I could do. It had been a fantastic experience and I had won just under £250. Johnny Miller became Open champion in 1976 winning the grand total of £7,500, not much by the standards of 2007!

It was hard to come down to earth after all that, but two weeks back at the club returned me to normality. My next event was the Midland Open at a new Shropshire course, Hill Valley, which was partly owned by Tony Minshall's dad, Albert. In a strong field I started well with 73 to be in fourth place, but followed with a disappointing 78 to finish 12th. After the tournament there was a big Pro-am featuring a number of leading players and after a good level par front nine of 36, I played great coming back in two under par 34, including a birdie on the difficult 18th. My 70 was good enough for second place and a £250 cheque.

The hot, dry conditions continued. I had a level par 71 in a Pro-am at Worcestershire and in the Second-City tournament at Sutton Coldfield I had eleven birdies in two rounds to score 72, 74. I entered the Sun Alliance match-play tour event, but failed to qualify at Gay Hill. By now it was September, and two more Pro-ams at Heysham and Hearsall were unsuccessful for me with 72 and 74.

It was about time I had another good score and it came in my next event, the PGA under-25's at Three Rivers, a new course in Essex. I played great in the pre-qualifying, hitting 15 greens and making five birdies to shoot a four under par 69, making me leading qualifier by two shots. In the tournament , playing the first two rounds with Howard Clark, I made a dreadful start with the putter, three-putting the first three greens and finishing on 80. After some hard work on the practice green, I came out the next day and used only 29 putts, nine less than round one, to make seven birdies and score 70, three under par. This was just good enough to make the cut and was followed by 74 and 75 to finish in 28th place, winning £63. Over the five rounds at Three Rivers I had made 22 birdies, but had also made too many errors.

I was invited to a Pro-am at Filton in Bristol and found the course to my liking, shooting a level par 70 on a windy day to finish second and win £185. My final tournament of 1976 was the Staffs and Shropshire Pro's Championship at Leek, where I played reasonably well in wind and rain for 73, 74 to finish ninth.

It had been a successful playing year for David Thorp. Over 46 tournament rounds I had averaged 74.2 and won nearly £1,500, equivalent to about £9,000 in 2008. I hadn't won any events but I had played in The Open and I couldn't wait for 1977.

04

158 ROUNDS IN 24 MONTHS

1977-AGED 23

My season started early in '77 with a Pro-am trip to Vale do Lobo on Portugal. I started well enough on the par-73 course but faded to score 73, 79, 80. It had been a nice warm-up for the bigger stuff to come.

It became clear that if I was to continue to pursue my tournament career, I would need an additional assistant to work in my shop. In those days of low wages it just seemed feasible, as long as I kept winning money, that it would work. A suitable candidate appeared in the guise of Brian Johnson, a good young player from Bideford in Devon. He and his younger sister played at Royal North Devon Golf Club and although Brian became a competent player, his sister, Trish was to be much better and has been one of Britain's most successful female professionals of recent years. Brian was to be a trusted assistant to me for the next three years.

I was off on safari again, but only for three weeks this time, which, in retrospect, was not long enough to get acclimatised. First we were Karen for a Pro-am where I scored a mediocre 76. Then it was Muthaiga for the Kenya Open. I knew the course well but always seemed to find the greens a struggle. I was beginning to notice more difficulty in swinging the club smoothly, I would sometimes get shaky and jerky and hit very poor shots. In the first round I was having those kinds of problems and took 79. My ball striking in round two was much better but 38 putts meant I took 75 to just make the cut. In the third round I stopped trying to read too much into the greens and had an amazing 26 putts to make seven birdies and score 67, the best round of the day! That night I was featured on local television highlights as they showed my birdie on the 18th. In the last round I was back to normal on the greens, taking 36 putts for 75 to finish 36th.

We then moved on to Lusaka in Zambia, a course I usually enjoyed. In the Pro-am I made a great start, playing the back nine first I had two-putt birdies on the par-fives 13th and 14th and a single putt birdie on the par-five 18th to turn three under par. Three-putting both the first and second greens set me back and I finished the round in level par 73, quite encouraging. The tournament began and I made only a fair start. I did manage to hit 13 greens but took 34 putts for 76, finishing on the ninth with a birdie two. At the start of the second round I was having terrible trouble swinging the club. I believe this was the dystonia becoming more apparent, but at the time I had no idea what was going on. It was very intermittent, so I tried to ignore it. The outcome was a 78, compiled with only 28 putts. Having just made the cut I hit the ball better in round three for a 75 to be in 46th place. The final round was another struggle and I finished on 77 to be 42nd and win £89.

Ndola was our final destination and I started the Pro-am well with a birdie on the first. I scored a one over par 74, which was a steady round. Round one of the Zambia Open was good, two under after five holes, I eventually finished on 72 to be in eighth position. I followed it up with a horrific round of 81 to go tumbling down the field. The third round of 78 was not much better to make me miss the 54-hole cut by two shots.

This time the Safari Tour had not gone well. I had won only a small amount of money and had made a loss on the trip for the first time. It was puzzling at the time that I could mix some very good play with spells that felt like I had never played before. However I wasn't deterred from my long-term goal of being a tournament star.

In April Rosie and I had a lovely holiday in Tenerife, almost getting away from golf! I had a game at the old Tenerife Golf Club and was made most welcome. I had two more really bad rounds in this month, 84 in a Pro-am at Hill Valley and 81 in a little event at Beau Desert, but then things began to improve again. On a cold, windy and wet day at Heysham, in a Pro-am on my old patch, I shot 72 to finish second and win £44 and in a small Pro-am at Coventry Hearsall I also scored 72.

Mid-May arrived an I was scheduled for an intensive spell of play with the Sun-Alliance match-play at Stoke Poges, the Penfold PGA Championship at Sandwich and the Midland Pro's Championship at Coxmoor all in consecutive weeks. The first two of the three events involved pre-qualifying, so there was no guarantee of my playing in all three.

I drove down to Beaconsfield Golf Club on Sunday afternoon hoping for a practice round in the evening before the qualifying the following day. I played round by myself and completely forgot I had nowhere to stay that night. By the time I came off the course it was dark and I noticed one of the players had a caravan in the car-park. He kindly asked me if I would like to sleep on his floor for the night and I gratefully accepted. He turned out to be Ian Woosnam and I don't think he goes to tournaments in a caravan any more!

The qualifying went smoothly, two under after four holes and finishing in level par 72 to get through with two shots to spare. On to the main event on the beautiful, tree-lined Stoke Poges course with its palatial clubhouse. In the first round I was drawn against South African Hugh Baiocchi, who was to go on to win the tournament. This was an unfortunate draw for me as I played pretty well but he played better. I had three birdies and an eagle and lost three and two, only winning two holes. There was no prize money for my efforts.

Down to the south coast next for the qualifying at Royal Cinque Ports, Deal, attempting to get through to Royal St. Georges. These two courses would turn out to be successful venues for me over the coming years. In windy and dry conditions at Deal I didn't make a great start, going out in 40 and making bogeys on ten and eleven, but then an excellent run of play got me home in 36 to be fifth best qualifier. Everyone had found it tough. The PGA Championship was the biggest tournament on the European Tour, and I was delighted to be involved, especially on such a great links as Royal St. Georges. Conditions were windy and dry throughout the week making scoring difficult. This is borne out by the fact that eventual winner Manuel Pinero scored 283, three over par. I started poorly with five straight bogeys to go out in 42. Somewhat better on the back nine, I eagled the 14th to return in 36 for a 78. Day two started promisingly with a par and a birdie and a front nine of 37. Another eagle three on the 14th and I was round in 73 to be in 54th spot. Disaster followed in the third round, taking 39 putts for an 81. On the final day I struck the ball well but took 37 putts to score 77. My 309 total put me in 65th position which unfortunately won no money. Interestingly, I was six under par for the par-five 14th hole, 'Suez', as it is known, with two eagles and two birdies. These two weeks had been costly but valuable experiences.

Before the Midland Pro's on Thursday I had to fit in a regional qualifying round at Rushcliffe Golf Club on Monday for the Club Pro's Championship at Hollinwell later in the year. Playing the course blind I did well to get round in 74 to book my place in the tournament. Things must have been very hectic at this time with a business to run as well but I seemed to manage it with help from Rosie and Andy. The Coxmoor tournament was played in some of the hottest weather I have ever experienced in England and the course was running fast. I played the 36 holes with Terry Squires, a great exponent of the Ping 1 iron off the tee, which was popular at the time. Making an excellent start, I was two under after nine only to finish level par on 72, in fifth position. A disappointing second round of 75 put me in ninth place to win £35.

Three minor successes followed. In a small Pro-am at Gay Hill my five-birdie round helped my team to first place and won me £106. I was runner-up in the Midland PGA par-3 Championship at Kings Norton winning £66 and achieved the most twos in the event, ten in all over the 24 holes. Playing blind in a Pro-am at the Cambridgeshire Hotel I shot 74 to finish fourth and win £100.

Then on June 29th at Great Barr Golf Club I played some stunning golf. It was an unusual 27-hole Pro-am sponsored by A1 paper. I started steadily enough on the back nine with six pars, and then eagled the 16th, parred the 17th and birdied the 18th to complete the nine in 34, three under par. Going on to the front nine I bogeyed the first, parred the second and then made four straight birdies. I parred the seventh then chipped in for a birdie on eight. A par three on the 9th meant I had shot 30 for the first nine holes and was now seven under par. A more normal, one over par nine of 38 completed my 27 holes in 102, six under par giving me a five-stroke victory. We were also joint-first in the team competition netting me a total of £350! My putter had been red hot, getting used only 38 times in 27 holes and I had made eight birdies and an eagle.

There was no time to celebrate as early the following morning I was driving up to the west coast of Scotland for the Open qualifying. After a brief evening look at the Western Gailes course my first round got underway at 2.10p.m. on July 1st in perfect weather. I made an equally perfect start with a birdie on the first and played steadily for 73 to be in 25th position. With 32 places available I was in good shape. With a morning time on day two we were suddenly faced with a strong wind and the course became a different proposition altogether. After making a great start, getting to one under at the third I had some ups and downs to finish in 77. My 150 total was looking promising until in the very last match, hours later, South African Bobby Cole beat it to eliminate those on my score. I was on my way home and could only watch enviously on television over the following few days, as Tom Watson beat Jack Nicklaus for the title in that famous 'duel in the sun' at Turnberry.

Following a few days at home I played in the regional qualifying for the English Open at Willesley Park. Not having seen the course before I got round in a very creditable one under par 69 to easily secure my place for later in the year. Just over a week later we had a Midland PGA tournament at the demanding Redditch course. Driving particularly well I had two rounds of 74 to finish fifth and win a small cheque.

Now that Rosie's school holidays had started she was able to travel with me and become my caddy again. We drove up north to attempt to qualify for the Newcastle Open. At Ponteland Golf Club I made a good effort but my 75 was two shots too many and back to Bridgnorth we came. A few days later in a Pro-am at Stanton-on the-wolds, again playing blind I managed seven birdies for a four under par 69 to finish fifth.

My first of many appearances in the PGA Club Pro's Championship was at the great Hollinwell Golf Club near Nottingham in mid-August 1977. Notts Golf Club, as it is also known, is a superb example of British heathland golf, but being longer than most, is a tough test. We had perfect, hot weather the whole week and Rosie and I worked hard to get a good result. I didn't get off to the best of starts with rounds of 78, 76 to be in 60th place, but things started to click into place with rounds of 71 and 72 bringing me through the field to 16th position. I had the best final 36 holes of anyone in the tournament and won £120. I had narrowly failed to make the PGA Cup team by just two shots.

The following week was the Second City tournament at Sutton Coldfield, another heathland course with which I would become very familiar over the next few years. This was one of the best Midland events at the time, with its own marquee, hand-painted score-board and much razz-matazz. The format varied over the years but it always caused much local interest. This year it was a 36 hole Pro's individual tournament on day one followed by a select Pro-am the following day, and I made a great start with a six-birdie round of 69, three under par to be in second place. A topsy-turvy second round of 77, containing two birdies and an eagle put me in 11th spot and booked my pro-am place. My team didn't do very well in the pro-am but I did win £50 for second shot nearest the hole on the 18th. Rosie had caddied again and we were becoming a good team.

After a couple of small Pro-ams the Midland Open was at Hill Valley in Shropshire, one of my local courses. I made another of my now regular fast starts when I chipped in for a birdie three on the third and hit a 5 iron to a foot for a birdie two on the fourth. Three more birdies on the back nine including another chip-in helped me to a 71 to put me in joint first place with Martin Poxon. A nice start to the second round put me one under after seven holes, but a poor run including five bogeys set me back. Pulling myself together again

I played the last four holes in two under par to finish in 74 for a 145 total, putting me in fourth position, just one behind the three joint winners. This was an excellent performance for me, but my winnings were only £80. A Pro-am followed where my team and I managed to finish first, ironically winning me more than I had made in the tournament.

Just three days later I was travelling again, this time to South Wales for a Pro-Am at Llanwern Golf Club, in the shadow of the steelworks. This was a disappointing round for me, because Rosie caddied and her parents, my in-laws came to watch me for the first time. I didn't play well, scoring 80 and became rather grumpy as a result!

The following morning (how I kept up with this punishing schedule I don't know) I was driving down to Laleham Golf Club in London for the pre-qualifying round of the TPD Championship. Later on the same day I teed off, never having seen the course before. A double-bogey seven on the first was hardly the ideal start, but I played well after that and got round in level par 70 to comfortably qualify. The tournament was at Foxhills, a demanding course that winds its way through dense woodland. A fine start had me one under par after five holes. A seven on the 12th spoiled things a bit but two further birdies gave me a one over par 74 and put me well up the order. A steady second round of 75 put me in 24th place, but a disastrous 84 in round three put me out of it completely. A final round 79 put me in 58th position, no disgrace, but just out of the money. Readers may find it hard to believe that I had played all four days in the PGA and TPD championships and had lost to the winner in the first round of the PGA match-play and yet had come away from all three events empty handed. These days I am sure that wouldn't happen.

Following two days at home I was again appearing in the Filton Pro-am in Bristol. Two under par after four holes I finished in 71 for fourth place, but was more proud of winning the £50 longest drive prize on the ninth for a smack of 320 yards! In those days I could hit the ball a fairly long way but there always seemed to be others who could hit farther.

Beginning on the 21ˢᵗ of September was the Rank Xerox English Professional Championship at the famous Sandy Lodge Golf Club at Rickmansworth, where previously John Jacobs had been professional. This was a new event carrying a prestigious title and I was keen to do well. I made the unbelievable start of birdie, par, birdie, eagle but the magic left me and I finished with 72, one over par. Another hot start of birdie, birdie was better consolidated in round two to produce a two under par 69. Lying in 18ᵗʰ place going into the third round I was feeling confident and managed another excellent start to be two under by the fifth, but then had an inexplicable collapse to shoot 75. Yet again getting to two under after six holes in the final round on a windy day, I held it together for a 72 to finish in 28ᵗʰ place with Tony Jacklin becoming the champion. My reward was a mere £83, not even enough to cover expenses.

There were a few more outings before the end of the year with mixed results but two of them were successful. In a small Pro-am at Lilleshall on a very windy day I finished top Pro with a 68, a new course record at the time and in a similar event at Dudley I shot a one under par 67 to come third.

The year of 1977 had been quite encouraging. I had played a huge number of rounds, approximately 87 in which I had a stroke average of 74.6, winning around £2,000. This was not a great return, but I felt I was still learning how to play in big tournaments and this knowledge had to be paid for. One high finish in a tour event and I could break into the big time! My back-up business at Bridgnorth was running smoothly and with Rosie's encouragement on and off the course, everything seemed to be in place for next year. The only worry was this strange problem of loss of motor control during my swing, but it only happened occasionally so I put it to the back of my mind.

1978–AGED 24

After a few rather uninspiring winter alliances, in late January I was off to Portugal for two weeks to play in Pro-ams. The first was at

Dom Pedro, a tricky course with a tree-lined back nine. I made a great start with a seven-birdie round of 68, four under par. This was a course record and gave me a three-stroke lead. My team also did well and we held a two-stroke advantage on the field. This wasn't to last and on day two I took 11 more putts than in the first round for an 81. In the third and final round I shot 76 to finish seventh and the team came in eighth. The following day I won a small stableford at the same course with 34 points. Then it was on to Vale do lobo for the second week where we were joined by a second Bridgnorth team captained by my assistant Andy. During a practice round on this very picturesque sea-side course I started feeling strange. I was shaky and weak and couldn't seem to hit proper shots or putt normally. Although it was intermittent and I still had some good spells of striking I scored a disappointing 77, 80, 81. Following the opening course record it had been a poor fortnight's play and had not been the confidence builder that I was hoping for.

In an alliance at Sandwell Park about a month later I had a really scary experience similar to, but worse than the one at Vale do Lobo. On the first hole I slightly mis-hit my drive but it finished OK on the fairway and then while trying to hit a seven iron second shot I was shaking badly and just couldn't control myself. After thinning it short of the green, I had an even worse time with the chip, almost missing the ball. I improved somewhat during the round, but I didn't know when it might happen again. It must have looked as if I was very nervous, but I wasn't, in fact I was always quite calm and confident. I decided to try and ignore it and it might go away, the old 'head in the sand' strategy!

My next outing was in mid-March at a wet, windy and cold Hill Valley where I scored a mediocre 78. The following week I was to play my first round in a Pro-am at the Belfry. It had opened in a flurry of publicity as a future Ryder Cup venue, but quite frankly it was dreadful! On a windy cold day it was a muddy mess and the fact that my 83 was good enough for sixth place and a small cheque tells its own story.

By late April it was still cold, windy and wet, conditions that have never suited me and I played in a Midland PGA event at another long, new course called Kings Norton. I struggled to 81,

77 and looked forward to better courses and nicer weather. By early May it was warmer but everywhere was still very wet and I was back on form with a two under par 68 in a Pro-am at Coventry Hearsall to finish third and win a small prize. Another promising round of 72 at the Peterborough Milton Pro-am a week later and my confidence was returning.

At the Shifnal Pro-am I had an excellent ball-striking round, hitting 15 greens and scoring 71 on poor greens to finish top Pro and win £93. Then in late May I attempted to re-join the big time in the PGA Championship at Birkdale. I was drawn at Southport and Ainsdale for the pre-qualifying, a venue I liked, but I never really got going and a 78 was several shots too many.

Following that disappointment it was back to the Pro-am scene at Oxley Park Golf Club. It was a warm June day and the greens were just right. Rosie was caddying for me and with a new putter and new putting grip everything felt poised for a good round. Hitting the ball superbly and putting well I made seven birdies, including three twos and shot six under par 65. This won by three shots and was a new course record, beating the previous best that had stood for 30 years, winning me £175. This was a great round and one that much enhanced my local reputation.

Several more Pro-ams followed, the highlight of which was a good ball-striking round at Moor Hall. Hitting 16 greens including two par-fives in two I had 35 shots and 36 putts for a 71 to finish third. The main event of the period was the Open at St. Andrews and for the first time the R and A introduced regional qualifying. I was at Beau Desert, a good heath-land course with notoriously tricky greens. The conditions were very windy, raining and cold, hardly ideal for July. I played reasonably well but couldn't hole anything and my 77 proved to be one shot too many, very disappointing. Jack Nicklaus was able to triumph at the Old Course without my challenge!

So it was on to the more mundane challenge of a Midland PGA tournament at Staverton Park, a course I invariably played well. Two solid rounds of level par 71 put me in sixth place, just two shots behind winner Ian Woosnam, netting £80. A couple of fair Pro-am rounds followed and then it was the Club Pro's Championship at Pannal Golf Club. This was a course I really liked built on rolling heathland and the first round was very much a family affair with Rosie on the bag and Mum, Dad and Brother Andrew walking round. I was pleased to play well and a five-birdie, four under par round of 68 put me in third place, one off the lead. I had mixed fortunes after that with 75, 77, 72 to finish 24th and win £62, small reward for a good performance.

I then played in the Midland Professional Championship at a very wet Ladbrook Park, and after a great start getting to two under at the third, shot two rounds of 74 to finish 15th. It was still wet for my favourite Midland event the Second City at Sutton Coldfield, but it was not to be a good one for me with rounds of 74, 76.

It was almost September and prize money was hard to come by, and then a nice level par 72 at the difficult Kings Norton put me second in a Pro-am, winning £135. Most welcome! Three more poor pro-am rounds were followed by the Shropshire Open, or Shropshire and Herefordshire Open as it is properly known, at Ludlow. I had lost in a play-off for this title in '75, but hadn't played in the event for the next two years due to clashing dates and knew it would do me a lot of good to win it. I played pretty well for 77, 71 to finish fourth, just two shots behind the winner. I don't know what happened to the prize fund, but I only won £8!

The Midland Open was also in Shropshire at Hill Valley, a course I was beginning to get to know but not particularly like. I played solid golf to score 73, 74, one over par and finish sixth, well behind winner Andy Griffiths, and won £55. In the post-tournament Pro-am I played very well to score a three under par 70 and finish third, picking up £134.

On October 3rd, playing the course blind, I played some great stuff in the Belton Park Golf Club's pro-am in Grantham. Hitting 15 greens, including two par-fives in two, I shot a three under par 69 to win by two shots. This was a course record and won me £120. Belton would turn out to be another of those courses that I invariably played well. I found it pleasing to the eye with its wide open spaces and herds of deer never far away.

One final event in 1978 was a very late European Open. There was a 36 hole qualifying tournament at Cuddington, in which I started with a birdie, but finished up with 72, 76 to miss out by six shots. A minor success in a winter alliance was recorded as follows in the local Express and Star " After more than 50 attempts to win a Staffordshire and Shropshire alliance, David Thorp from Bridgnorth finally succeeded at Hawkstone Park yesterday when he and his partner returned a winning 66." The partner was my good friend Richard Mobberley who more than played his part!

Things were changing at the club. Rosie and I had decided it was about time we bought our own house and I had enquired how much extra retainer I could have should we choose not to live in the club's house. The answer came back as £5 per week, which would take my retainer from £15 to £20 per week. This was very disappointing, so I began to look for a move. After four years my assistant Andy had by now become PGA qualified and in December moved to Ludlow as Professional, leaving me with just Brian.

Golf-wise, the year was mixed. Some brilliance with three course records, but I had not qualified for any Tour events and my only good finish in a big tournament had been 24th in the Club Pro's. I had played 71 rounds including alliances with a stroke average of 74.4 to win £1,500. I felt that the muddy winter conditions and long spells on temporary greens at Bridgnorth had not helped my golf, so a high quality course was a pre-requisite for my new club.

05

BRITS ABROAD

1979-AGED 25

Early 1979 was very cold with ice, snow and sub-zero temperatures lasting weeks and weeks. No golf was being played and business was non-existent. Jack Hargreaves was retiring as Pro at Sutton Coldfield and I had applied for the job. On a wintry January 17th I arrived for my interview and by the end of the day I had accepted the position to start on March 1st. Due to the weather I was unable to play the course, but I knew it well and loved its springy turf and fast greens. This would be the ideal place to develop my game. The members were keen for me to play and the retainer was more than double that at Bridgnorth. Brian was keen to come with me and I agreed to also take on one of the existing assistants, Charlie Dicks. We were also soon to discover that Rosie was pregnant, so it was just as well that I was going to make more money!

Before getting the job, I had arranged a two-week Pro-am trip to Portugal, so away I went. I played steady, if not spectacular golf to score 73, 76 at Vale do Lobo in a rain- affected event and 76, 75,

74 at Vilamoura. I won some prize money but not enough to cover expenses, as was often the case in foreign Pro-ams.

Bridgnorth Golf Club was sorry to see me go, and my successor was Paul Hinton, son of the Pro at Enville. Paul and his wife Angela were to become good friends of ours and have remained at Bridgnorth until 2007. The new club was very helpful and supportive in all departments, and soon Rosie and I moved into a flat in Aldridge, overlooking a development of new houses, one of which we were going to buy on completion.

My new shop at Sutton was nothing fancy, with rather unattractive rubber matting on the floor, but it was an improvement on the previous one, and over time the club upgraded it for me. The outgoing pro Jack Hargreaves was a rather dour man, typical of his generation of professionals, and had been a successful player, getting selected for the 1951 Ryder Cup team, but incredibly was not given a single game. Jack won many titles in Warwickshire and in 1953 won the then vast amount of £500 in beating Roberto de Vicenzo to take the Swallow Match-Play tournament. He also had been PGA captain in 1977 and wished me well as he left Sutton after 32 years in the job. I remember a comment he made when I asked his views on the future of the club professional, "Doomed", he said. A little over-pessimistic, I thought!

The weather was still poor in March and a small tournament had been unwisely scheduled for the Belfry on the 28th. I played in atrocious conditions and started suffering badly with my movement problems. I really struggled to control my swing and compiled an 87, embarrassing in the extreme, especially since I was playing with old Lancashire pal Nigel Sumner. It was starting to get me down but I battled on. In April we had the Midland Pro's Championship at Lincoln, a good course I hadn't played before. I started well with 72, but a second round 80 demoted me to 30th. In the Pro-am that followed I was six over after 10 holes and then played the last eight holes in three under par for a respectable 73.

In late April I was lucky enough to play in a 36-hole Pro-am at Sunningdale, undoubtedly one of the great places to play golf. A first round of 77 on the New (due mainly to taking 38 putts) was followed by an encouraging 71 on the Old, containing four birdies and an eagle. No prize-money was won but it was just a privilege to play there.

On April 29th it was the Jack Hargreaves Testimonial Pro-am at Sutton. There was a strong field and, with this being the first big event at the club since my arrival, I was keen to do well. I made a fine start, getting to two under par after eleven, but three subsequent bogeys gave me a 73 and 10th position, no disgrace. Three more pro-ams followed soon after without success, but the 75 I had at Stourbridge was notable because it was made up of 36 shots and 39 putts. An unusual statistic, but I had noted that the greens were bad on the day, undoubtedly due to the poor Spring weather.

Rosie and I had a very welcome holiday touring the West Country in late May, leaving the assistants in charge. Everything was still there on my return and on June 4th it was the Midlands regional qualifying round for the State Express Pro-am at the Belfry. My partner was Bob Fletcher, an affable fellow-Yorkshireman who was a teacher. Bob had qualified in a designated competition at Sutton and should we win we would qualify for the national final in Portugal in November. I hadn't enjoyed my two previous visits to the Belfry, but it was better this time although still wet under-foot. I played very well to be round in 71 and Bob did his bit to give us a better-ball 68 to make us the winners, but there was a problem, Bob couldn't go to the final, as it was in term-time. With the PGA's permission a replacement was found with the unlikely name of David Weatherhogg. My prize on the day was £210, but I did feel sorry for Bob.

After a few average results I started to play better. On a windy day in the Gay Hill Pro-am I shot a level par 72 to finish second and win £100, then two days later I was at a 36-hole Midland PGA tournament at Staverton Park. After a rather shocking start of six, six to be three over after two holes, I played some great stuff to score 72, 68 for a two under par total of 140. This put me in seventh place, seven behind winner Ian Woosnam and netted £76.

In early July it was time for The Open again. It was at Royal Lytham this year and I desperately wanted to play since I knew the course so well. I first had to get through the regional qualifying at Beau Desert where I had narrowly failed last year. In dry and windy conditions I was out in 36 and looking good but suddenly had a bad run. A good two-putt birdie four on the 18th gave me a 76 and I had to wait to see if that was good enough. In the end it was, but only after a sudden death play-off where I got through with a par on the second. Then I had the great news that I was drawn on St. Annes Old Links, scene of many good rounds when I was assistant at Fairhaven. I knew I could get through there if I played my normal game and I would be able to stay with my parents and brother at Wharles in their new home not far from Lytham.

Playing with another former local boy Peter Wilcock and with my 16 year old brother Andrew carrying the bag, we set off in rather wet and windy weather. I made a great start by holing a long birdie putt on the first and went to the turn in 34, two under par. Two bogeys and a birdie coming home and I was round in a fine 71, which put me in seventh position. There was to be about 18 qualifying places so I was looking good. Round two, in better conditions didn't start so good and with three bogeys and six pars I was out in 39. Then, playing solid golf I made eight pars and a birdie on the last for a 74. My 145 total was good enough by one shot and I was an Open Championship competitor again!

On Tuesday evening Rosie came up by train to give me support. Unusually for The Open the weather at Lytham in 1979 was wet, windy and cold which made scoring very difficult. I had a nice draw for the first two days with two Englishmen who I knew, John Harrison and Peter Mitchell. The first at Lytham is a long par-three of 206 yards, unique among Open courses and my 4 iron tee shot missed the green to the right. I chipped up to eight feet and knocked it in for an opening par. Playing pretty well round the front nine, but only managing to hit four greens in regulation I was out in 37, not too bad but now I had to face the fearsome back nine which was playing mostly into the wind. Starting back with two nice pars, I then hit one of my best ever shots in The Open. The 12th is a tricky par-three of 201 yards and the pin that day was on the right edge of the green surrounded by deep bunkers. With a hard left to right wind I hit a perfect 2 iron with just enough draw to hold it up and it finished three feet past the hole to set up an easy birdie. Five more pars followed but then I found trouble on the 18th to make a double-bogey six. My 74 was still a good score and by the end of the day I was in 25th place. The back nine had played so difficult that although I had hit the ball well, I had only hit two of its greens in regulation. I was pleased to have played it in 37.

Day two, Thursday was even colder than the first day and still the wind blew. I made a nice start after just running through the back of the first green with my 5 iron, chipping to four feet and holing out for a par. A good drive down the second left me with a 9 iron to the green, which I hit to 10 feet. A successful putt put me one under but it wouldn't last. With the course playing so tough sub-par rounds would be very rare indeed today, and after playing the next four holes in four over par my score was slipping. Then, just at the right time I staged a recovery. On the par-five seventh I hit drive, 3 wood, sand wedge to six feet and holed it for a birdie. The 394 yard eighth was playing very tricky; the tee-shot was OK but the down-wind second shot to the firm, elevated green was one of the hardest shots on the course. After a good 1 iron off the tee, my wedge second shot looked perfect but it didn't hold and went over the back. A great return chip to three feet saved the par. The short ninth plays into the far corner of the course and was playing very short. A perfect 9 iron to 10 feet was followed by another single putt and I was out in 36.

A solid par on 10 was followed by a great birdie on the par-five 11th. Back into the wind, 11 was playing long, and after successfully avoiding the huge fairway bunkers off the tee, I hit a 3 iron up the middle and a superb punched 7 iron to 15 feet and again holed the putt. I was back to level par for the round and plus three for The Open, almost on the leader board! Three good pars in a row and I reached the 15th tee. This 468 yard par-4 was into the teeth of the wind, and after hitting a solid drive my 1 iron second shot came up short. A chip to six feet, but this time the putt missed to give me a bogey five. A regulation par on 16 and it was on to the 17th, the famous Bobby Jones hole, an immensely hard par-four, dog-leg left. A good drive missed all the threatening pot bunkers and my 1 iron second missed the green right. I played a fine chip to six feet but again the putt stayed out, another bogey. On to the 18th with its massive grandstands and thousands of spectators. A very tough drive into the wind had to avoid the horse-shoe of deep bunkers and fortunately mine did. I still needed a 2 iron and just pushed it a bit to find one of the bunkers on the right. I played out to 15 feet and my par putt agonisingly lipped out. I had finished in 74 again and my 36 hole total of 148, six over par, put me in 31st position. Over the two rounds I had used only 55 putts and had hit only 14 of 36 greens in regulation. The course was playing very tough and I had done well. I was ahead of many good players, including Peter Oosterhuis, Ray Floyd, Sandy Lyle and Johnny Miller. I was tied with Nick Faldo but instead of getting drawn with him I was to play with American star Hubert Green, who had famously won the 1977 US Open despite receiving a death threat on the last few holes. He was also destined to win the 1985 US PGA Championship and to be a three-time Ryder Cup player with an excellent record of four wins.

Hubert was an unorthodox player with very low hands and a fast swing. His putting style was also unusual with a very crouched posture, but I knew he would be a good player and I didn't want to put him off. The third round was on Friday. It was another cold and windy day and again I was trying to get used to playing among golf's elite. Nick Faldo had just gone off in front of us and Tony Jacklin was two matches after. Hubert was off first and the starter Ivor Robson introduced him as US Open champion of just two years earlier. He surprisingly missed the par-three first green and then it was my turn! I don't remember what introduction I was given but there I was on the tee with a 5 iron. I made a nice swing and hit the green about 45 feet from the hole. I two-putted and was off with a par. A good drive down the second was followed by an excellent 8 iron to 25 feet and two putts for another par. Bogey five on the difficult third was followed by a solid par on the fourth and I was feeling OK. On the 212 yard par-3 fifth, it was my honour and after extensive consultation with my caddy Andrew, I decided to hit 6 iron. Addressing my ball, something didn't look right and after checking the sole of my club I discovered I had a 9 iron in my hands instead of a 6 iron, a visual error familiar to all hackers! This caused much good-natured amusement to Hubert and our sizeable gallery but I wasn't unsettled. I eventually bunkered it left, then splashed out to 12 feet and unluckily lipped out. The next hole is where the occasion started to get to me. On the par-5 I kind of zig-zagged my way down the hole and with having to move ropes and people I sensed I was delaying Hubert, who was a fast player. I managed to complete the nine in 39, which wasn't disastrous, and I could still make the 54-hole cut with a half-decent back nine. A par on the tenth was followed by bogeys on 11 and 12, a par on 13 and a bogey on 14. I could still play the last four holes in one over par and make the last day but it wasn't to be. The wheels came well and truly off and I finished in 84 to miss the cut by five.

I apologised to Hubert for my performance and he was very nice, saying that you have to get used to playing in big tournaments to be able to play well in them. He had played steadily apart from a double-bogey six on the 15th where he unwisely tried to hit a driver off the tight fairway grass and thinned it into a cross-bunker, and finished with 73. My other memory of him is hitting sand-wedge chips from behind his right foot that barely got airborne but came to an abrupt halt after two or three bounces. In the long-term my confidence had received a small boost by the realisation that I could hit the ball just as well and equally as far as a world-class, major-winning player. It had been another great Open Championship adventure that won me just £300 but provided more lasting memories. Seve Ballesteros finished up as champion, famously playing his second to the 16th from a car-park on the right. Some of his tee-shots were wild but he was a deserving winner.

It must have been hard to come down to earth, but it was back to the club for the week-end and then off again to the Club Pro's Championship at Pannal on Monday for a Tuesday start. In warm conditions I played consistently but took too many putts to score 73, 74, 73, 72 for 292, the same score as last year but this time finished 35th, 11 places worse than in 1978. A couple of welcome tournament-free weeks were to follow, much-needed I am sure.

I returned to the fray for the Nuneaton Pro-am on Sunday August 12th. In good conditions I made the ideal start, holing a long birdie putt on the first and continued to play well, making five birdies in all to shoot a two under par 69 and finish second pro, one shot behind the winner. Back at the club the preparation for the Second-City tournament was well underway and I was very confident of a good result on my home course, which, as always for this event, was in the peak of condition. The 36-hole pro's competition was on Wednesday, the first day and suddenly the weather had become very windy, wet and cold. In these conditions Sutton would be a tough challenge with its thick rough and firm ground. Starting early in the morning I bogeyed the easy first, parred the next three and then birdied all three of the consecutive par-fives, five, six and seven. Par on the eighth and a three-putt bogey on the ninth put me out in 36, one under par. This was a great start because the wind was now gusting up to an incredible 50 miles an hour, blowing the scores sky-high. Putting was becoming increasingly difficult and with 19 putts on the back nine I came home in 38 for a 74 to be jointly in the lead. I had hit the ball superbly in this round, finding 16 of 18 greens in regulation and hitting all but one fairways off the tee. Starting on the 11th in the afternoon round I made a bad start, but recovered somewhat towards the end for a 78 to finish in third place and win £170.

The big Second-City Pro-am was on the second day and to everyone's relief, the weather had calmed down somewhat. I had a good range of handicaps in my team with a lady off three and two men off four and 15. There was no individual competition, the prize-money was all for the team event and the format was the best net score of the four of us on each hole. I played great golf all day and in the first round hit 17 greens in regulation, made four birdies and was round in three under par 69. My partners all contributed to a tremendous score of 61, which placed us third at the half-way stage. Coming out after lunch I got off to a dream start, after a perfect drive down the first, my 50-yard sand-wedge pitch second shot landed just right, gripped and released straight into the hole for an eagle two! On the short second I hit a nice 9 iron to 10 feet and holed that for another two. My partners then took over for a few holes, but I was back again with successful birdie putts from short range on eight and nine. Another birdie on the difficult 11th was followed by yet another on the 13th and we were flying. We eventually finished with 60 for the second round for a remarkable total of 121, 23 under par and were victorious by three shots. Personally I scored 69, 66 to be nine under par, one of my best ever performances. I had won £425 to go with my £170 from the first day, a fantastic tournament for me on my home course that attracted a lot of local press coverage. It was great that Rosie had been able to walk round part of the way, even though she was very pregnant at the time!

Over the next couple of weeks I played in four small Pro-ams, the best of which was a fine one under par round of 69 at Droitwich where I came in fifth. We then had the Midland Open on the formidable Redditch course, with its fearsome back nine. My two over par first round of 74 was full of ups and downs and contained no less than six birdies, putting me in seventh position. Round two was a very solid affair, hitting 16 greens and missing just one fairway, but unfortunately taking 36 putts for 73. My total of 147 was good enough for third place and a cheque for £332, a pleasing result.

On September 4th I again played in a 36-hole Eurogolf Pro-am at Sunningdale, which was fast becoming one of my favourite courses. I shot a 74 on the New, then a gratifying 69 on the Old. Very little prize-money was involved but I felt playing there was an essential part of my golfing education. The following day I was at a Pro-am venue as different to Sunningdale as could possibly be imagined, Dudley Golf Club in the heart of the Black Country. Describing the Dudley course is difficult; some of its most memorable features for me are the dangerous blind shots hit over hills where you know there is OB quite close but you can't remember exactly where! Strangely, it has always seemed to suit my game and this day was no exception, in windy conditions I compiled a six-birdie, one under par round of 67 to win the Pro's event and just under £100.

My punishing schedule continued the very next day with the 36-hole Warwickshire Open at Leamington. Starting with a one over par 73 I went into lunch in seventh spot. Playing the back nine first in the afternoon, a two on the 11th got me to one under par, then bogeys on 16 and 17 were followed by a birdie three on the18th to be out in 35. A superb back nine of 34 containing six pars and three birdies gave me a 69. My two under par total of 142 was good enough for third placed Pro and a £100 prize. I was on a run of fine form.

The following week we had the Midland PGA match-play championship at Burton-on-Trent Golf Club. At this stage in my career I was inexperienced at match-play, unlike some of my colleagues who had played amateur golf, but over the subsequent years I was to become strong in this form of the game. The course was playing well and the greens were running fast. In the qualifying round I hit the ball superbly, but took 38 putts to score 75, fortunately good enough to progress to the match-play stage for the leading 32 players. My first round match was against Glen Clark, and again I struggled on the greens, three-putting five times, but I just came out on top by one hole. In the second round against Nick Ryan I played well to be level par and prevailed again by just one hole. During this match I holed a 40-yard sand-wedge shot for an eagle on the third. In the quarter-final against Chris Holmes, I holed a long birdie putt to win the first and on the seventh holed a full 9 iron for an eagle two on the way to being seven up after nine holes. I eventually won 7&6 or by a 'dog licence' as it used to be known. I was feeling confident going into the semi-final, but ran into an in-form Andy Griffiths. Despite making three birdies I went down by 5&4 and Andy went on to lose the final to Richard Livingston. There was a third-place play-off for me against Glyn Stevens, which I won by 3&2, winning £190. That same afternoon I had to go out again in a post-tournament Pro-am at Burton, in which I scored a creditable 73. It had been seven rounds in four days, more than enough golf for anybody!

Rosie was now due to give birth to our first child very soon so I stayed close to home and cancelled some appearances. I did, however play in a small Pro-am at Boldmere, the short municipal course almost next-door to Sutton, and managed to win the event with a course record 63, even though it was one over par. Playing the course blind, I hit 16 greens in regulation and came back in 29, my first time under 30 for nine holes. On the 25th of September our new daughter Emily Kate joined the human race. I was, unfortunately, playing golf at the time, having been told to go away by the medical staff, but got back to the hospital soon after the event and all was well.

A week later and I was back in action again at the Warwickshire match-play championship at Stratford-on-Avon Golf Club. Richard Livingston, Pro at Ladbrook Park and myself were both in the field and since Richard had just become Midland match-play champion and I had finished third, we were both fancied for the title. I quickly decided that I liked the course and won my first match 6&5 against

Graham Taylor, making five birdies and an eagle in the process. I showed similar form in my afternoon game against John Gould, winning 6&4. A great semi-final followed the next morning against David Steele, a renowned long hitter. Three down after 11 holes, I played some solid stuff to eventually come out on top by one hole and would meet Richard Livingston in the afternoon final. In front of a sizeable local gallery, I played level par golf for 16 holes but lost 3&2. It had been another good match-play performance for me, being approximately seven under par for my four matches and losing only to the Midland match-play champion.

Soon after I was at a Pro-am at Hill Valley in Shropshire and produced a superb ball-striking round of 70, two under par, hitting 15 greens and 13 of 14 fairways to finish second pro and win £130. The following week I drove all the way to Felixtowe for a 36-hole tournament. An excellent three under par 69 put me in fifth place after the first round, but a poor 77 dropped me to 21st and out of the money.

The home tournaments were coming to an end now, but I wasn't finished yet by any means. Playing the tricky Cosby Golf Club for the first time in a Pro-am I hit 16 greens to score a one under par 70 to claim third place. Then on the 30th of October I was invited to a rather exclusive Pro-am at Hawkstone Park Golf Club with a very strong field of mostly Tour Pros including Sandy Lyle who had grown up at Hawkstone. On a cold and wet autumnal day I played well to shoot a one under par 71 and finish third, one ahead of Sandy. I only won £95, but my confidence had received another boost.

In early November I was lucky enough to escape the dreary English weather for a week at Penina in Portugal for the final of the State Express Pro-am for which I had qualified at the Belfry earlier in the year. My stand-in partner was David Weatherhogg, a good single-figure player, as original qualifier Bob Fletcher was unable to go. Penina was a long and difficult course lined with tall trees, designed by the legendary Henry Cotton. It was also wet and was playing extra-long this week. There was no individual competition, but there was an excellent prize fund for the better-ball score. We made a great start in the first round with a four under par 69 to be in third place out of 16 teams. I had been two under myself and

David had also played well. Our second and third rounds were disappointing, 72 and 71, largely due to my poor play. My partner had held things together well and we finished 11th I had, however, made nine birdies in three rounds on a long and tough course, which was some consolation. We had been very well looked after by the sponsors in the superb Penina Hotel and I hoped to qualify for the event again in the future.

All that was left now in 1979 was a couple of winter alliances, which was a rather unappealing prospect after the excitement of Penina. One of them, at Stratford on December 6th, did produce some excitement. Partnering high-handicap Sutton member Richard Langley, I went round in 68 and due to some amazing play by Richard we had a better-ball of 61, 11 under par! Needless to say, we won the day.

So that was it, another enormously busy year of playing, with some pluses and some minuses. I played 84 competitive rounds with a stroke average of 73.5 and won over £3,000, about £12,000 in today's money, my best figures yet. I had played in The Open for a second time and had made the 36-hole cut again. My swing had held up well, largely self-maintained and apart from some bad trouble early in the year, the dystonia had not bothered me much. The big negative was that I had played too many Pro-ams and not enough big tournaments. This was largely a matter of convenience as I could be there and back in the day and still keep in touch with what was happening in my shop and could get home to see the family. But playing with three amateur partners who often didn't take it as seriously as me and who sometimes didn't even realise that I was trying to win the Pro's medal was not good for my development. I needed to get back on tour sooner or later if I was to fully realise my potential.

Our happy domestic life was suddenly in turmoil when Rosie became ill. A headache deteriorated to the point where an ambulance had to be called and she was hospitalised. With baby Emily only three months old, this was traumatic all round. She was diagnosed with encephalitis, a swelling of the brain that can be very serious. Mother-in-law came to stay and between us we looked after Emily. This went on throughout the Christmas period and it was several weeks before Rosie was given the all-clear to come home. I had become quite adept at giving the baby her bath!

1980–AGED 26

Following Rosie's illness, I didn't play anywhere for a couple of months, but my first outing was a pleasant surprise when I went round Moor Hall in a two under par 68 in an alliance in March. My business was then thrown into disarray when Brian Johnson, my assistant of three years, decided to leave at the end of March. Brian and Charlie had run the shop well during my frequent absences and it would not be easy to replace Brian. The shop had done reasonably well for me in my first year at Sutton, nothing spectacular but together with my retainer it had given me a steady income to allow me to chase my dream as a player, which had been the plan from the start. Brian's successor was to be Tony Goldingay, a pleasant local lad of small stature whose game was never quite good enough to become a Pro, but would be a reliable assistant in partnership with Charlie Dicks.

In late March I went out to Spain for the Midland PGA Pro-am at Las Brisas and Aloha. Las Brisas had held golf's World Cup in 1973 which had been won by the formidable partnership of Jack Nicklaus and Johnny Miller. It was a long, testing course with lots of water. I made a great start getting to four under after nine holes at Brisas, eventually finishing in a two under par 70, putting me in first place by a shot. On day two, in windy conditions, a 77 on the same course put me in third place, just one off the lead. The final round was at Aloha, a hilly course with some of the fastest greens I had ever experienced. I played well to score 71, one under par, to finish second to Jim Rhodes, winning myself £190, probably not enough to break even for the trip, but a very encouraging performance, nevertheless.

So much for getting back on tour! In April I only played three competitive rounds, all in Pro-ams, but two of them were quite significant. On the 10th I went to another 36-hole Eurogolf Pro-am at Sunningdale. Playing the New, starting on the 11th in the first round I made a great start, birdieing my first two holes. Things cooled down a bit after that, but on the fourth hole, a longish par-four to an elevated green something amazing happened. Following a perfect drive I was left with an uphill second shot of about 195 yards into a stiff breeze to a pin that was only just visible on the top level at the back of the green, a very difficult ask. I then proceeded to hit a perfect 1 iron that finished in the hole for an eagle two! I have holed a lot of shots in my career, but on reflection I think this was the best. I finished the round on 71, one over par, in third position. After a nice lunch in the historic old clubhouse it was onto the Old course for the afternoon round. It was to be a superb ball-striking round marred by taking 38 putts, but my 74 together with the morning's 71 was good enough to take first place and £85. Over the entire 36 holes I had not missed a fairway and to win even a small event on such a great course was a thrill.

I then had a couple of really bad Pro-am rounds where I was struggling to control my movement, particularly with the putter. It was embarrassing, since I looked as if I was nervous, with my tremulous efforts, but, in fact I was very confident in my abilities and it was all very frustrating. At this time, these spells came and went and by mid-May I was getting back to normal again. On a very hot day in the qualifying round for the Club Pro's championship at Northants Golf Club I comfortably got through with an unimpressive 75 and could look forward to the final at Turnberry later in the year.

The very next day I had a 12.30 tee-off time at Royal Cinque Ports, Deal, on the south coast, in the pre-qualifying competition for the PGA Championship at Royal St. Georges. I had played Deal three years earlier when I successfully got into the same event. In contrast to the day before, Tuesday May 20th was cold and windy at Deal and I played steadily for a 74 to qualify by one shot. I was delighted to be again competing with the elite on a championship links for the first time since the Lytham Open last July. Having had two days solid practice I was ready to perform in the first round on Friday, but St. Georges proved to be a fearsome test in cold, windy conditions and 79 was the best I could manage. Saturday's weather was still testing and although I hit the ball well, 37 putts contributed to a 76 which meant I missed the cut by four shots. Nick Faldo was champion with the unusually high score of 283, three over par, which shows how tough it was. One happy note for me was my continuing love affair with 'Suez', the par-five 14th at Sandwich. In 1977's PGA

I had played it in six under par with two eagles and two birdies and this time I had made a birdie and an eagle to be three under for the two rounds. It was fast becoming my favourite hole!

A couple of unsuccessful Pro-ams were followed by the Midlands regional qualifying round for the State-Express national Pro-am, the event I had won last year which took me to that nice week at Penina in November. My partner from Sutton was Joe Fisher, a steady single figure man who was well suited to the tight Beau Desert course. We combined well in the four-ball format to score 65 and finished second, just one agonising shot behind the winners. No Portuguese trip this year but a consolation prize of £136.

So far this year had been rather up and down, unusual for me and I couldn't understand it. I then had a poor run of scores in various events- 80, 77, 80, 75, 79, 77. A fine one under par 71 at Shirley in the second round of the Warwickshire Pro's championship broke the sequence, but I was very shaky and out of control and decided I should seek medical help. I arranged to see my GP who was sympathetic but couldn't seem to understand what was going on, so I just carried on. Rosie and I then went to Bournemouth for a week's holiday with the baby and Rosie's parents. We all shared a flat and had fun, I think, but I do remember Emily crying a lot!

Playing in a Pro-am at Redditch on our return, I had a fortunate result. Scoring only an average 76, I finished second individually and brought in the winning team to win £240. Would this spur me into form? I was hoping so, because next it was The Open at Muirfield. I was to play Luffness in the qualifying. Being a relatively easy course, low scoring was expected. So it proved on a benign first day, when I shot a respectable 71 to find myself in 40th place. In contrast, it was very windy and cold for the second round and the scoring soared. This invariably happened when the weather changed at The Open. The foreign players, such as Americans and Japanese, tended to struggle in wind and rain on links courses. But 77 was the best I could manage, and I failed to qualify by just four shots. It had been a reasonable performance but having played two Opens I badly wanted to play again.

Just after The Open I won my first Midland PGA tournament as opposed to Pro-ams. "Thorp's success comes out of the blue" was the headline in The Birmingham Post. The venue was Rushcliffe Golf Club, a rather hilly course I had never seen before and I was using a new, light-weight Ping Anser putter. I played great all the way round for a five-birdie 67, three under par, to win the 18 hole event by one shot, and a cheque for £285.

My confidence was now renewed somewhat and in late July off I went to the west coast of Scotland for the British Club Professional's championship at the renowned five-star Turnberry resort. I was a little disappointed to find that we weren't going to play the famous Ailsa course, but instead the tournament would be on the Arran course, slightly inferior but still a good test. I always relished links golf in windy conditions, and fancied my chances if conditions stayed the same throughout the week. On a very blustery first day I made a great start with a 73 to be lying third, just one off the lead. For the second round we were off very late in the afternoon after a rain delay and since it was wet and windy, visibility became poor. All the other groups finished their rounds but one of my partners, veteran tour player Hedley Muscroft, complained that he could no longer see where he was going, so we were told to walk in and had to complete our last four holes the following morning. That didn't bother me too much and I finished in 76 with just 12 putts on the back nine. Day three was very windy and my 72 was a fine effort which put me into ninth position. Another solid 72 in the final round for a total of 293 put me joint seventh, seven shots behind winner Dave Jagger, and made me £300 richer. More significantly, I had qualified for Great Britain and Ireland's nine-man PGA Cup team to meet the USA in Oklahoma later in the year. I couldn't wait!

Several more small Pro-ams followed with mixed fortunes. The best results were two rounds of level par at Ladbrook Park and Nuneaton and then in mid-August it was again time for the Second City tournament at my own club, Sutton Coldfield. I was really anticipating a good performance here, as I normally played Sutton very well and I had been in the winning team last year. As usual it was the pro's 36-hole event first and in good, but showery conditions I played great in the morning round. On the front nine I hit every green including the par-five seventh in two to be out in 34, three under par. Coming back I took three putts for a bogey on the 12th

The 1980 PGA Britannia Cup Team

Back (left to right): Peter Harrison, Tony Minshall, David Talbot, David Huish, Jim Farmer, Alec Bickerdike.
Front: John McTear, David Jagger, Leonard Owens, David Thorp.

Newly qualified 1980 PGA Cup team, Turnberry, Ayrshire (thanks to PGA).

and made another bogey on 16. Then a birdie two from close range on the 17th and a par on 18 meant I was round in 70, two under, to be in second position. In the afternoon I didn't play quite as well for 73 for a one under par total of 143 to finish fifth, good, but a little disappointing. In the team competition the next day we combined well to score 63, 62-125 to finish second. Over the two days I had won £300, very pleasing.

The good results I had achieved were being noticed increasingly, particularly in the Birmingham Post, where I would regularly be praised, but in truth my form was patchy due to this wretched problem of going weak and wobbly when I swung or putted. It was intermittent and when I was unaffected, things were great and I could compete with anybody, but when it was bad the ball could go anywhere. I saw my doctor again and he recommended a hypnotherapist in Sutton Coldfield, so I made an appointment.

Pro-ams at Copt Heath and Hill Valley produced indifferent scores of 74 and 77, with only one birdie in the two events, but then things improved again. In a Pro-am at Llanwern in south Wales I made two birdies and an eagle for a two under par 71 to finish fourth. A four-birdie 72 at Droitwich was followed by a five-birdie 72 at Glen Gorse. Small cheques were won in each case. Next we had the Warwickshire Open at Edgbaston. I played steadily but lost a ball on the 12th in round two and scored 71,73 to finish fourth and win £65. Two days later in a Pro-am at Sandwell Park, one of the best courses in the Midlands, I got off to a great start, four under par after 11, but fell back to score level par 71, finishing fifth.

I then had the first of nine hypnotherapy sessions with a mysterious Dr. Anderson. They were bizarre experiences that didn't seem to have any effect and cost me a lot of money, but it seemed like I had to try something. Just one more event was scheduled before our exciting American trip, and that was the Midland Open at the difficult new course, Forest of Arden. In windy weather I played reasonably to score 74,78 and finish 12th. Not great, but I felt fairly good going into the PGA Cup match.

The 1980 PGA Cup was a really big deal for me, to become an international player and represent my country was going to be incredibly exciting and I couldn't wait! Rosie was going with me, as were most of the wives, and her Mum and Dad were going to baby-sit Emily at our house. On Monday September 15th we departed on a big orange Braniff Airways jet destined for Oklahoma City via Dallas. All our team members wore their official PGA blazers and ties. It felt just like being in the England football team travelling to the World Cup! While in transit at Dallas airport it was amazing to see so many huge people with the men all seeming to wear cowboy boots and stetsons. The American hospitality was tremendous; in the hotel we had our own team room complete with our personal country singer to keep us entertained. Throughout the week we had dinner engagements all over the place nearly every night. The wives had their own bus to take them to various activities including taking part in a live daytime TV chat show and were treated like royalty!

The golf was the main thing, of course, and the team had to get to know each other, partnerships had to be formed and we had to familiarise ourselves with the course and the conditions. David Talbot was our captain, a fine player himself, he did his best but we only had three days preparation, which was nowhere near enough. I knew all of the team and had played with most of them over the previous few years. We had some good players including Dave Jagger and David Huish who were successful tournament winners. The Oak Tree course was like nothing I had ever seen before. Designed by Pete Dye and over 7,000 yards long, it had lots of water holes and fast, undulating greens. The holes varied in style and were intended to mimic several different famous courses around the world. Oak Tree had only been open for four years and was already in the USA's top 50 courses. It was incredibly difficult and was destined to hold the USPGA Championship in 1988. To add to the test, we had temperatures in the nineties all week with intensely bright sunshine and a very strong, dry wind. These were very unfamiliar conditions to most of our team and definitely affected some of the British players. We were warned about scorpions and snakes and told not to venture into ditches to retrieve balls. Local caddies were allocated to us and Rosie walked every hole down the side-lines with the other wives.

After two practice days both teams played in a Pro-am, before which was a lavish opening ceremony complete with piper, dancers and speeches to introduce the teams. In the Pro-am I hit the ball well and putted well to score 76, which doesn't sound impressive, but such was the severity of the course that I finished seventh Pro and won £70, only two shots behind the winner, our own Dave Jagger. This was a good result and helped to get me selected for the first series of four-ball matches the next morning. The format was such that only six out of nine players on each side would compete in each of the four series of games on the first two days, then everyone plays singles on the final day.

The American team was largely unknown to me, but they had to be good since they were the top nine out of 1,400 entries in the US Club Pro's championship and our side was the top nine out of a mere 300 entrants for the British equivalent. They didn't do too well in the Pro-am so maybe they weren't so hot after all?

In the first round four-balls I was paired with Tony Minshall, the youngest member of the team, from Hill Valley in Shropshire against Buddy Whitten, the American Club Pro's champion and George Shortridge. In hot and very windy conditions, we were second match off, and it was quite a moment when the starter said "Representing Great Britain and Ireland, David Thorp". I hit a decent drive, as did Tony, and we were away. Tony made a superb birdie three on the tough 441 yard first hole to put us in the lead, a dream start! Halving the second with a par, we lost the third to a birdie and the fourth to a par. Two halves in par were followed with a win for us, by me with a par four on the 440 yard seventh, named 'Dye's dread'. Back to level, but not for long as they won the eighth with a birdie and the ninth with a par. USA two up at the turn. Halves in par on 10 and 11 were followed by my winning birdie three on the 445 yard 12th. The 13th was halved in pars and Tony then proceeded to hole a long winning birdie putt on the 14th to take us back to all square. Whitten holed from 12 feet for a birdie on the long par four 15th and we were one down with three to play. The 16th was a par five of only 479 yards, but a stream meandered up the middle of the fairway and to the left of the green, making it tight. Both Whitten and I were on the green in two, but he was much closer than me. I putted up close to make my four, but he holed his seven-footer for a winning eagle. Dormie two down, but anything could happen on the 200 yard par three 17th with its big lake extending from the tee right up to the fringe of the

A hot, windswept practice range at Oak Tree, Oklahoma, USA, 1980.

PAIRINGS AND STARTING TIMES 1980 PGA CUP MATCHES

Saturday Results — USA 9½; GB & I 2½

SUN., SEPT. 21 — A.M., BEST-BALL MATCHES

GB & I		USA
1. 10:00 a.m.		
D. Jagger	vs.	J. Lewis
2. 10:10 a.m.		
D. Huish	vs.	T. Florence
3. 10:20 a.m.		
J. Farmer	vs.	G. Shortridge
4. 10:30 a.m.		
T. Minshall	vs.	R. Glover
5. 10:40 a.m.		
L. Owens	vs.	D. Barber
6. 10:50 a.m.		
D. Thorp	vs.	R. Kennedy
7. 11:00 a.m.		
A. Bickerdike	vs.	D. Campbell
8. 11:10 a.m.		
J. McTear	vs.	T. Aycock
9. 11:20 a.m.		
P. Harrison	vs.	B. Whitten

NO CAMERAS ALLOWED

Final day drawsheet, PGA Cup, Oak Tree, Oklahoma, USA, 1980.

green. I managed to hit the green and make three, but they made a two to win by three and one. We had played well to be two under par, but they were a magnificent five under for the 17 holes of the match. I was particularly pleased to be two under par for the last eight holes.

We had lost all three morning matches by small margins and over lunch the afternoon pairings were revealed. I was delighted to be selected again but a little dismayed to be partnered by David Huish, one of the few of our side that I had not played with and being much older than me, our paths had not crossed much before. In foursomes against Tommy Aycock and Doug Campbell we just didn't gel and went down five and four. This was very disappointing and I feel sure I would have played better with Tony Minshall or Peter Harrison, both of whom I knew well. In foursomes you need a comfortable rapport with your partner, and David and I didn't have it.

Not surprisingly, I was dropped for the morning fourballs on day two, but was out there again for the afternoon foursomes with Tony Minshall against Tommy Aycock and George Shortridge. The team was down seven-two at this stage so we needed to play well. We made a nice par on the first but the opponents birdied and we were behind already. Several holes changed hands and the USA were two up at the turn. The back nine was an amazing roller-coaster ride of wins and losses and after finding ourselves three down with four to play, we won 15, 16 and 17 with a run of par, birdie, par to stand on the 18th tee all square. Neither side played the last hole well and in the end Tony holed a gritty six foot putt for a bogey five to halve the match. Our half-point was the team's only success that afternoon and we would go into the last day's singles nine and a half-two and a half behind, still in with a faint chance. It had been a thrilling match to take part in and Tony and I had combined well.

For the final day, I was drawn against Roger Kennedy, a tall, 38 year-old club pro from Florida, and was determined to do my bit for the team. I bogeyed the first to go one down, but then had a great run of three straight winning pars to be two up after four holes. Losing the sixth to a par, I then won seven, eight and nine to be four up at the turn. Winning the 10th with a par four, I found myself five up with eight to play, a seemingly comfortable position, but then Roger made a come-back, winning 12, 13 and 14 with pars and 16 with a birdie. My five hole lead had been reduced to one on the 17th tee, but fortunately Roger missed the green and I hit a superb 2 iron over the lake to within 20 feet of the hole. Two putts later I had won the hole and the match by two and one. I was one of only two British winners in the singles and we lost to the USA 15-6 overall. We had a nice dinner in the evening where all the players and wives from both sides mixed and chatted cordially.

My overall performance was pleasing in the hot and windy conditions, particularly my putting. I played all through without a three-putt which was unbelievable on such fast and sloping greens, and my one and a half points was the joint highest total achieved by anyone on our side. After playing Oak Tree, most of the English courses were going to seem easy and I was looking forward to some good play on returning home. I did struggle, at times, with muscular control and found it awkward to explain to one of the American team why I shook and wobbled when he asked about it.

Arriving at Gatwick at 7.15 a.m. on Tuesday 23rd of September after an overnight flight and feeling jet-lagged, Rosie and I made the long drive home and were delighted to get back to little Emily, just two days before her first birthday. I was entered in a Midland tournament the next day but had to withdraw due to exhaustion!

I had recovered sufficiently by the following Monday to play in the Warwickshire match-play at Stratford. Everything pointed to a successful tournament for me here, and so it was to prove. My first round was against big-hitting David Steele and in heavy conditions he had a distinct distance advantage, but I was on top form. Hitting every green on the front nine and only making one single putt I turned one up. Still one up with three to play, I won the 16th with a par three and the 17th with a birdie four to go through three and one. Second round opponent was John Gould, an up and coming young player. I struggled on the front nine greens; they were so much slower than Oak Tree, and was one down after nine. Playing the back nine in a three under par 34, with five single putts, I just came out on top in a very close game by one hole. The semi-final and final were both to be played on the Tuesday and my next opponent was Ray Leach, one of the least fancied competitors. Things didn't start according to plan for me, however, when I lost the first two holes to pars by missing consecutive short putts. I pulled them back and by the turn I was all square again. A holed bunker shot for a birdie two on 10 and I was one up. Two further birdies on the 13th and 15th and I had won the match four and three.

I was to play Phil Weaver in the final and was determined to win this time after being losing finalist in '79.

Phil was a fine player who had played on tour and was a prolific winner of Warwickshire events, so I knew I would have to play well to come out on top. We set out in perfect conditions and after hitting my second shot close on the par four first, I holed for a winning birdie three. He won the third, fifth and eighth while I won the fourth, all with pars, and Phil was one up after nine. Then I suddenly went into a different gear and had a great spell of play. I was hitting a hard fade all week and on the back nine it worked particularly well. On the par three 10th I hit it close to make a winning two to square the match. On the par five 12th I hit the green in two and two-putted for a winning birdie to go one up. The next four holes were halved in par and on the par five 17th, after hitting the fairway off the tee, I hit a nice 2 iron onto the green and two-putted for a birdie to win the match two and one. I was the 1980 Warwickshire PGA Match-Play Champion, which got my name on a trophy and won £200.

I was on a real high now and couldn't wait to play again. The Belton Park Pro-am was just two days later and I knew I would be hard to beat. In a superb ball striking round where I hit every fairway and hit 15 greens, including six times inside 15 feet, I was unlucky to be only one under par with a 70. However, it was good enough to win first prize by one shot and I drove home from Grantham £150 better off. The weather was starting to turn and my season was coming to an end apart from a few Warwickshire Alliances, which I always found rather unexciting.

The golfing year of 1980 would have to go down as very memorable, with some strong form shown late in the year. Playing in the PGA Cup and becoming Warwickshire match-play champion would be the highlights. I had played 61 rounds and averaged 73.8, winning over £3,000, similar stats to last year, but fewer events played. I still needed to play more big tournaments against top opposition. This would be in my plans for next year.

06

Best In The Midlands

1981–AGED 27

My season started early with a trip to Portugal in mid-January for a 54-hole Pro-am at Vilamoura with some regular partners of mine. It was cool and windy and the par 73 course was a stiff test. I made a fast start, getting to two under par after just four holes, but it wouldn't last. Multiple bogeys took me to four over after 12 holes, but then a solid finish, culminating in a nice two-putt birdie on the 18th gave me a 76 to put me in fourth position, just two off the lead. Following putting troubles on the front nine in the second round, I played the back nine in two under par for a 75 to put me third going into the final round. Round three began perfectly with a par four on the first and a great eagle three on the second. Bogeys on the sixth and eighth put me out in level par 35, in good position for a high finish. A bad collapse on the return nine, apart from a birdie on 18 gave me a disappointing 77. However, I still finished fourth and won £237, probably not quite enough to break even on the trip.

I had decided to go to the Safari Tour again as part of my plan to compete at a higher level. The prize-money had increased and if I could reproduce my form of late '80 I could do well. I would only go for three weeks; one in Kenya and then two in Zambia. This would be my fifth African trip and even though I had missed the last three years, I knew the courses and many of the people well.

We started at Muthaiga in Nairobi with its mystifying grainy greens. I played steadily in the Pro-am with a 73 including five birdies. Encouragingly, I hit three of the par-five greens in two shots which proved I was swinging well. Conversely, I made a very poor start to the Kenya Open with a six over par 77, which gave me a big task just to get through the cuts after two and three rounds. Round two started a little better and I went out in 37, one over. Finally, my game came back with four birdies on the back nine for a round of 70, putting me in 45th position. My third round was another lacklustre affair finishing in 75 to drop to 47th, but at least getting into the final round meant I would be in the money. The fourth round got off to a poor start with a first nine of 39, but then coming back I hit every green in regulation, making seven pars and two birdies for 33 to make a 72. I finished 43rd and won £292. I had struggled with my movement control and my confidence had taken a hit, but at least I had finished strongly and set off for Zambia hoping for better things.

Arriving in Ndola, I was again staying with a nice Scottish couple, Bob and Margaret Hughes and we started with two pre-tournament Pro-ams, and after a good start in the first one, I fell away badly for a 79, but I wasn't really concerned. I was better in the second Pro-am with a one under par 72 including three consecutive birdies on the back nine. The main event got underway and I was really struggling to swing smoothly. If I hadn't had eight single putts, my 78 would have been much worse. On day two I was completely different, only missing two fairways and two greens. The only blemish in my level par 73 was to three-putt three times. The third round was fairly steady with two birdies and three bogeys for 74. In the final round I couldn't swing again on the second nine and did well to keep it to 75. My 300 total was not good but I did win £294 for 35th place.

On to Lusaka for the Zambia Open. The course was playing nicely and I thought that if I could avoid these nasty shaky spells, I could finish well here. In the Pro-am I hit the ball superbly, hitting

16 greens and 13 of 14 fairways. The putting was not so hot, however and I shot a 75. The first round got going and my good play continued, making four birdies in the first 13 holes to be two under. A bogey on the 17th gave me a 72, one under par and 16th position. Round two was another excellent performance with four birdies and two bogeys for a 71, still 16th. The third round brought more of the same. A mere 27 putts enabled me to amass five birdies and just two bogeys for a 70. This was great stuff, 213 for 54 holes, six under par and 14th position. The standard dropped in the final round, unfortunately and only hitting 10 greens in regulation I scored 77. My total of 290 was still a fine two under par and gave me 27th place and a cheque for £521. It had been a good tour and winnings of £1,100 in three weeks meant a healthy profit. At the end of March I was confident of a good year's playing ahead.

Around this time one of my assistants, Charlie, decided to leave. He had been a loyal member of staff, but I think he realised he would never make the grade as a professional player, and opted to move on. His successor would be Ian Neal, a good golfer, and although a little rough around the edges seemed like a suitable replacement.

There wasn't much playing in April. It must have been prudent to spend some time at the club after having been away so much. In early May I went down to Stoke-by-Nayland in Suffolk for a 36 hole tournament. My 76, 75 was a very average effort and I finished 13th, winning not much!

Then it was back to the big time with the pre-qualifying for the Martini at West Hill, a lovely heathland layout in Surrey that I took an instant liking to. Playing the course blind I scored a level par 69 to be third best qualifier. The main event was at the famous Wentworth, which I hadn't played before, but knew well from televised tournaments that I had watched. A good opening 73 put me in 25th place and only four shots off the lead, but the wheels came right off on day two. Although good off the tee and hitting 11 greens, I took 37 putts and scored 82. A 78 would have made the cut but as it was I was off up the road with no winnings.

On the 20th of May we had a Pro-am at Shifnal on a very wet Wednesday. The conditions didn't seem to bother me and I shot a one under par 70, including six birdies, to finish top Pro and win

£160. Two days later and it was the Warwickshire Professional Championship at Finham Park, Coventry, a good par 73 course. Phil Weaver and I renewed our county rivalry. Phil scored 145 on his home course to win by two shots and I was runner-up with 74,73-147. I hadn't hit the ball great but had putted well with totals of 29 and 30 and my reward was £150.

The day before that last event we had an early morning call to say that my father had died in his sleep of a heart attack. He was only 54, but had suffered heart trouble and the stress of financial problems for sometime and had not been fit for several years. It was still quite a shock and I had gone up to Lancashire to be with Mother and my 18 year-old brother Andrew. I decided to go ahead and play at Finham and it was remarkable that I did so well under the circumstances. The funeral was in Lytham the following week. It was a sad affair, but I took a set of my old irons to give to my brother to try and cheer him up a bit. He had now become a very good player and had got down to two handicap at Fairhaven. Doing his 'a' levels and hoping to go to university in the Autumn, this must have been a troubling time for him. Mother subsequently managed to get a council house in Lytham, where she still lives today, and was able to move away from the rather isolated village of Wharles.

It was back to business the following week with another foray into the big time. The Lawrence Batley tournament was at Bingley St. Ives Golf Club, but first I had to pre-qualify at Keighley. Playing the course blind, I didn't really get going until the back nine when a run of three consecutive birdies on 11, 12 and 13 set me up for a level par 69 which was good enough to get through. I now had got the hang of these qualifying rounds and was developing a good success rate. If only I could carry that form throughout the whole tournament.

On a very windy day, I got off to a horrific start in the tournament proper, two double bogeys put me four over after only two holes. Through all this trauma, something happened to one of my playing partners that was so tragically comical that it was hard not to laugh. His identity escapes me, but on the par-five second he was on the green in three and faced a long birdie putt. His caddy attended the flag and as his putt approached the hole I could tell it would be close.

The caddy wrestled with the flagstick as the ball neared the hole, but it wouldn't come out. As his heaving now became desperate, the flag came out and so did the cup, just in time to knock the ball out of the hole as it tried to go in! The player couldn't believe his eyes as the ball came to rest about three feet from the hole. Once the cup had been re-inserted, he inevitably missed the short putt and what should have been a four became an unlucky eight, with penalty shots included. Golf can be a cruel game! My round never really recovered from that start and I shot 80. Day two was a similar story for 10 holes but then four birdies in the last eight holes, including three in a row on 14, 15 and 16 cheered me up a bit and gave me a respectable 75. In difficult conditions the scoring had been high and my 155 total only missed the cut by five shots.

The following week, on the 9th of June, it was again the Midland regional final for the PGA's national Pro-am with its final again at Penina in Portugal. This time with a new sponsor, '3 5's'. This had been a great event for me, having won the qualifier and gone to Portugal in '79 and finished second in the 1980 regional final. We were again at the Belfry, scene of our victory of two years ago. The course was fast improving and was due to host a tour event later that summer, and would hold the first of its Ryder Cups in 1985, just four years from now. This being a better-ball competition, my partner would be all-important and the club's qualifier was Doug Hands, a steady player around the eight handicap mark. On a windy day the Belfry was a stern test and the scoring would be high. I played some outstanding golf, especially on the back nine where I birdied the 11th, 12th, 13th and 15th to score a personal 71, two under par. Doug played his part and our score of 69 beat the rest of the large field by three shots. I won £237 and once again we were booked for the Portuguese final in November.

Later that month was the Midland Professional Championship at Burton-on-Trent. Two years earlier I had finished third in the Midland match-play here, so I knew the course well. Not feeling quite 100%, with a touch of flu, I battled round on the first day in 75 to be lying 20th. On day two, feeling better, I made five birdies but could only manage a 73 to finish 11th. In the post-tournament Pro-am, however, I played very solid golf, hitting 15 greens and scoring level par 71 to finish fourth. Over the three days I won about £120, not too bad.

The fortnight beginning July 6th 1981 I had ear-marked to be a significant turning point in my career, when I was going to prove that I could perform on the big stage, and partially that is what happened. The first part of my plan backfired badly. The English Classic was the first tour event at The Belfry and since I had just recently had an excellent 71 there in the '3 5's' Pro-am, I was confident of a high finish. Conditions were blustery for the qualifying round and scoring was difficult, but after 13 holes I was only two over par and looking good, but a series of disasters followed and I finished on 78, one shot too many to get through.

Gutted about failing at The Belfry, I would have to wait a week before playing again in The Open qualifying. Another opportunity came up that week with an invitation to a small Pro-am at Patshull Park in Shropshire. Playing it for the first time, I enjoyed the course, making five birdies for a one under par 71 to finish fourth.

On the Friday, off I went to The Open. Determined to give myself a good chance, I would have Saturday to practise at Royal Cinque Ports, Deal, my qualifying venue. Just the previous year I had successfully got through to the PGA Championship at Deal with a 74 and in 1977 I had done the same with a 76, so I knew what to expect. It was a great, classic British links with lumpy fairways, deep bunkers and little protection from the wind blowing off the English Channel. It had twice held The Open in the distant past and was just the kind of course I enjoyed. On a breezy first day I set off in great style. Hitting all the greens in regulation on the front nine, four times inside 15 feet, I turned in three under par 33. With eight pars and a solitary bogey on 16 coming home I was round in a two under par 69 and lying sixth, a superb start. Day two was windier which made the course a harder proposition. I played steadily, avoiding major disasters and got round in 75. My 144 total put me on the last score among the qualifiers, but there was one player too many, so the four on 144, including myself, would have to go out for a sudden-death play-off in the evening.

Just one out of the four of us would be eliminated. Play-offs are always nerve-wracking affairs, but for a place in The Open that would be an enormous under-statement. The first hole at Deal is a straight par four of around 400 yards with the clubhouse on its right and a wide ditch across the fairway just in front of the green. As with most holes on the course, there is a carry of some 150 yards over thick rough to reach the fairway. The first man to drive was an Argentinian named Molina. To my surprise, he nonchalantly tossed his ball onto the tightly cut turf without using a tee and proceeded to top his 3 wood into the rough in front of the tee! The rest of us all safely hit drives down the fairway, and were surely thinking that we would be the qualifiers and our South American colleague would be eliminated. However, golf is not that simple and he played a fine recovery down the fairway just beyond our tee shots. Mine was the longest of the three drives on the fairway and after the other two had hit the green, I caught my 9 iron a little heavy and, just carrying the ditch, finished on the front of the green, a full 45 feet from the hole. Mr Molina proceeded to hit his third to about six feet and then it was my turn again. I hit a lovely long putt that finished about a foot away and I was able to tap in for par. As it turned out, Molina holed his par putt, one of the others two-putted for par and the fourth player, who had hit two nice shots onto the green, three-putted to be eliminated. His disappointment was short-lived, however, as he became first alternate and eventually got in when one of the competitors withdrew.

I was to play in my third Open, this time at Royal St. Georges, Sandwich, a course I already knew quite well, which contained my favourite hole, 'Suez', the par-five 14th, for which I was currently nine under par for six rounds. Could I keep it up? My brother, Andrew was to make the trip to Kent to caddy in his third Open and it would be great to renew the team again. We were lucky enough to find some very cheap digs in Ramsgate, where we happily stayed for the whole week. Unfortunately, Rosie could not make it this year, but followed my progress closely from home in Aldridge.

The Open was now starting on Thursday, with a Sunday finish, so we had Tuesday and Wednesday to practise. The course was in excellent condition, but the weather was very mixed and it didn't seem likely to be one of those scorching Opens. I didn't play great in the practice rounds and the highlight was probably having a snack with Tom Watson in the tea-room and sharing an interesting conversation. He has always been one of my favourite players, with his no-nonsense style and superb swing. On Wednesday afternoon I was working hard on my swing on the range when John Jacobs came along the line of players as he liked to, and since he had helped me in the past, I asked him if he would take a look at my swing. He kindly agreed and before long came up with the advice that I should turn my shoulders on a more horizontal plane and swing my arms in a more vertical one. That really hit the spot and I started nailing one shot after another down the middle. I would carry this swing thought through the week.

For the first 36 holes I had a nice draw with Englishman David Russell, who I already knew quite well and South African Mark McNulty, a fine player who would turn out to be a big money winner in the future. Starting out in the morning, we had a stiff westerly wind but I started in fine style hitting a perfect drive down the centre of the severely undulating first fairway. A nice iron to the green and two putts later I was away with a par four. Another regulation par at the second was followed by a superb birdie two from close range at the difficult 214 yard third. The following few holes proved very tough, three pars and three bogeys were the best I could do, to go out in 37. The next four greens were hit in regulation, but a three-putt on the par three 11th meant I was three over after 13. Surely I would birdie the par-five 14th, my favourite hole in tournament golf! Not this time, a nasty double bogey seven put me five over par with four holes to play. Good pars on 15, 16 and 17 kept me at that mark on the 18th tee. The last at Sandwich was a hard 458 yard par-four, which I could only bogey to give me a 76, six over par. As the day wore on the weather deteriorated to the point where the late starters had to play in heavy rain. Jack Nicklaus was one of those off late in the day and he would take 83, one of his worst ever scores in The Open. My 76 was not looking too bad, only six off the lead in 59th place, ahead of players such as Faldo, Price, Trevino, Player, Stadler and the great Nicklaus.

Day two was on Friday 17th of July. Our group was off at 1.20 and the conditions were cool but less windy. Mark McNulty had scored 74 in the first round and David Russell 79. I was in between with

Scorecard 1

✓ 74
✓

148

110th OPEN GOLF CHAMPIONSHIP
SANDWICH

Friday 17th July at 1.20 p.m.

Competitor: Mark McNulty   Game No. 34

Hole	Length in Yards	Par	Score	Hole	Length in Yards	Par	Score
1	445	4	4 ✓	10	375	4	4 ✓
2	376	4	4 ✓	11	216	3	3 ✓
3	214	3	3 ✓	12	362	4	5 ✓
4	466	4	4 ✓	13	443	4	5 ✓
5	422	4	4 ✓	14	508	5	5 ✓
6	156	3	2	15	467	4	4 ✓
7	529	5	5 ✓	16	165	3	3 ✓
8	415	4	4 ✓	17	425	4	6 ✓
9	387	4	5 ✓	18	458	4	4
Out	3410	35	35	In	3419	35	39
				Out	2410	35	35
				Total	6829	70	74

Signature of Competitor: *Mark McNulty*
Signature of Marker: *David Thorp*

Scorecard 2

59.

69

110th OPEN GOLF CHAMPIONSHIP
SANDWICH

Friday 17th July at 1.20 p.m.

Competitor: David Thorp   Game No. 34

Hole	Length in Yards	Par	Score	Hole	Length in Yards	Par	Score
1	445	4	4	10	375	4	4
2	376	4	3	11	216	3	3
3	214	3	2	12	362	4	4
4	466	4	5	13	443	4	4
5	422	4	4	14	508	5	4
6	156	3	3	15	467	4	6
7	529	5	4	16	165	3	2
8	415	4	4	17	425	4	5
9	387	4	4	18	458	4	4
Out	3410	35	33	In	3419	35	36
				Out	3410	35	33
				Total	6829	70	69

Signature of Competitor: *David Thorp*
Signature of Marker: *DJ Russell*

Scorecard 3

73.

152

110th OPEN GOLF CHAMPIONSHIP
SANDWICH

Friday 17th July at 1.20 p.m.

Competitor: David J Russell   Game No. 34

Hole	Length in Yards	Par	Score	Hole	Length in Yards	Par	Score
1	445	4	4	10	375	4	4
2	376	4	4	11	216	3	4
3	214	3	3	12	362	4	4
4	466	4	4	13	443	4	4
5	422	4	5	14	508	5	5
6	156	3	3	15	467	4	5
7	529	5	4	16	165	3	4
8	415	4	4	17	425	4	4
9	387	4	4	18	458	4	4
Out	3410	35	35	In	3419	35	38
				Out	3410	35	35
				Total	6829	70	73

Signature of Competitor: *DJ Russell*
Signature of Marker: *Mark McNulty*

Second round scorecards, Open at Sandwich, Kent, 1981 (thanks to R&A).

76. I made a great start with a regulation par-four on the testing first hole, and a birdie three on the 376 yard, dog-leg left second. On the long par-three third, just like in the first round, I hit a long iron close and made the putt for a two. The fourth is a 466 yard par-four with a massive bunker to clear off the tee and as on Thursday I struggled to make a one-putt bogey. A solid run of regulation play gave me four pars and a birdie from close range on the par five seventh to be out in a superb 33. Starting back I continued my steady play with four pars and then a birdie on the 508 yard par-five 14th (my favourite hole) to be three under par with four holes to play. A double bogey six on the treacherous 467 yard 15th slowed me down a bit, but then on the 165 yard 16th I holed a 36 foot putt for a birdie two. A bogey five would follow on the 17th, but then an excellent up and down for a par four in front of the grandstands on the 18th enabled me to shoot a 69, one under par, my best ever score in The Open. Mark McNulty scored another 74 for a 148 total, I was 76, 69-145 and David Russell shot 73 for 152, which missed the cut by two. I was delighted to have beaten them both so emphatically.

My five over par score for 36 holes put me in 20th place, just seven shots behind the leader, and eventual winner, American Bill Rogers. I had some very high class company on the score-board with Nick Faldo and Nick Price sharing my score, Sandy Lyle and Arnold Palmer one behind, Seve Ballesteros two behind and Jack Nicklaus four behind after a superb second round 66. Andrew and I eagerly awaited the third round draw, and when it was published, I was excited to be paired with young South African star Nick Price.

There were 81 players in Saturday's field, and that number would be reduced to 60 for the final round. We teed off at 1.15p.m. in warm and breezy conditions and I hit another great drive down the long par-four first hole. I followed it with an equally good 4 iron over the cross-bunkers to about 10 feet, and proceeded to knock in the putt for a birdie three. What a start! After solid pars on two and three I then made my third straight bogey on the difficult fourth. Four more pars would follow and then a superb birdie three on the 387 yard 9th where I hit a 9 iron second shot to six feet. Going out in one under par 34, I was edging up the leader board. Things didn't go quite so well on the back nine; bogeys on 10, 13 and 18 and another double bogey on 15 combined with pars on the other five holes to give me a 40, for a total of 74. This was two shots better than Nick Price and my 54 hole score of 219 had me in 35th spot going into the final round of the 1981 Open Championship. It was like a dream, Andrew and I were having a great time and I am sure we both wondered if I could keep up this form to the end. Again we couldn't wait to see who I would play with on Sunday. It turned out to be Australian Rodger Davis (famous for his plus-twos) and we would have Jack Nicklaus and partner in front, and Arnold Palmer and Greg Norman behind. I was hoping I wouldn't hold them up!

I became a little nervous on the first tee on Sunday when I realised that I would be following the great Jack Nicklaus round the course and would see at first hand how he played in the situation he relished, the last day of a major championship. Conditions were again windy and the course would continue to be a difficult test. Once Big Jack and his entourage had cleared the fairway, Rodger drove first and when it was my turn I hit my fourth consecutive perfect drive down the first. A great second shot within 15 feet set me up well for a birdie but I would two-putt for par. A steady par four on the second was followed by a poor run of bogey, par, bogey, bogey. A birdie four on the seventh was followed by more bogeys on eight and nine. My front nine of 39 was by far my worst of the week and I was now faced with the tougher back nine, which I had played in 39, 36 and 40 in the previous rounds. I really scrambled for my score on the return half, managing a 38 with just 14 putts. I will never forget playing the 18th in front of packed grandstands, hitting a drive and one iron just left of the green and getting down in two for my par. My 296 total put me in 50th place. Rodger shot 74 with a disappointing double-bogey on the last. Jack Nicklaus finally overtook me with a last round 70 for 290.

My final position was joint 50th, which won £550, plus a bonus of £150 from Titleist for playing their ball, one of the few occasions when a golf company paid me for using their product. This performance was great for me in many ways. It was the first time I had played The Open without my game falling apart and my golf had compared well with my partners. In round three, I had beaten Nick Price, who would go on to be a fantastic player and world number

Last round drawsheet, Open at Sandwich, Kent, 1981 (thanks to R&A).

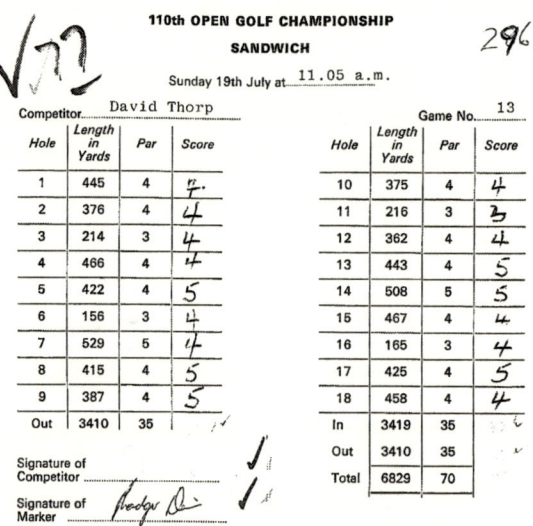

Last round scorecard, Open at Sandwich, Kent, 1981 (thanks to R&A).

one for 44 weeks, by two shots and I had led the great Jack Nicklaus for three rounds. I really should have continued to play tour events while I had the momentum, but I had been away for 10 days and was missing Rosie and Emily as well as feeling some responsibility to spend some time at the club.

As it turned out, I didn't play for a fortnight, but when I came out again the force was still with me! In the Midland PGA Match-play at Staverton Park, I just scraped through the qualifying in a sudden-death play-off after a 73 and then had an amazing first round match with Alistair Malcolm. Playing some of my best golf to date, I won the last four holes to win one up. The statistics of my round make impressive reading; putts-32, shots-34, greens in regulation-18/18 (including seven times within 15 feet), drives in fairway-11/14, birdies-five, pars-13, score-66 (five under par). Alistair also played superbly and was very unlucky to lose, but that's match-play!

In the second round against Kevin Hayward I continued to play well, birdieing the last two holes of the match to win four and two, to be three under par for the 16 holes played. For the next morning's quarter-final against Pip Elson, the weather changed completely from hot and dry to constant heavy rain. We had a very close game with Pip eventually coming out on top on the 23rd. I had again performed solidly, but Pip was one of the best putters I ever played with and the short stick was really working for him that day. There was still one more round to play at Staverton in the post-tournament Pro-am. Again I played superbly, only missing two greens in regulation, but taking 36 putts restricted my score to 72. I had been approximately five under par for my five rounds at Staverton and was swinging superbly, but my reward had been a mere £135.

Just before embarking on another adventure in the big league, I played in a small Pro-am at Blankney Golf Club in rural Lincolnshire and had another successful day. Playing the course blind, I hit 15 greens in regulation and scored a one under par 69 to finish third individual Pro and helped my team to win the Pro-am event to win over £200 in total.

On Sunday August 16th I drove up to Leeds to stay with my Auntie Kathleen to have another crack at qualifying for the Benson and Hedges at Fulford in York, an event I dearly wanted to take part in. I was again on Strensall for the pre-qualifying, as I had been on the three other occasions I had tried and failed to play in this prestigious event. I played solidly for a 71 and managed to get through a sudden-death play-off to qualify successfully. I was delighted to finally get to play at Fulford, a course I felt I already knew through the annual TV coverage of the tournament. With such a strong international field the scoring was bound to be low so I couldn't afford any slip-ups.

I did not make the best of starts in the B and H with a lacklustre 74, two over par and was in danger of missing the cut. Round two was one of those up and down, roller-coaster rounds where I had a six and a seven offset by six birdies, two of them in the last three holes. It all added up to 73, which just made the cut on the bubble. My third round started in fine fashion reaching four under par after 12 holes taking me briefly below par for the tournament, but it didn't last and a 71 for a 54-hole total of 218 would put me in 40th place, alongside Nick Faldo, going into the final day. Sunday's round started well with a fine birdie three on the long par-four first and a birdie two on the third. Things deteriorated subsequently, but I rallied at the end to birdie 17 and 18 for a 73. My three over par 291 total put me in 50th place, tied with Howard Clark, and won £345. Nick Faldo had accelerated away from me with a 67 to finish 29th. The great American player Tom Weiskopf won the Benson and Hedges by one shot from Bernhard Langer and Eamonn D'Arcy with a score of 272, 16 under par. His prize was £15,000, a meagre amount compared to the first prizes of 2008! Mine had been a pleasing performance, in very high-class company. I had pre-qualified, made the cut and continued to play well through to the end, just as I had done recently in The Open.

From York on Sunday night, it was down the M1 to stay with friends Lesley and Stephen for the Club Pro's Championship at Woburn. In the pre-tournament Pro-am after starting poorly, I had an encouraging three under par back nine of 34, which concluded with a holed wedge shot from 60 yards for an eagle two! Great things were expected of me in this event but, as often happens when you are hotly tipped to do well, the opposite happened. I liked the tree-lined course, but it was fairly new and not yet in the best of condition. In the first round nothing went right for me and my 81 looked like ensuring a missed cut. The following morning I packed my cases and said goodbye to my hosts, expecting to be on my way home later that day. Instead I shot a superb two under par 70, one of the day's best rounds, to just make the cut, and that evening returned to my somewhat bemused friends for two more nights! Rather untidy rounds of 75, 77 followed to put me in 45th position.

With just one day back at the club to do all my paper-work and catch up with events, I was off again on Sunday to a Pro-am at Leamington Golf Club, a bit closer to home. I played a very solid round, using my putter only 29 times to score a four under par 68 to finish second and win £182. If only I could have shot some 68's in those recent big events!

On Wednesday the inaugural 1981 Telford Ironmasters got underway on a course that would be significant for me in future years. Playing the Great Hay course for just the second time, I took a liking to it and shot 72, 70 for a two under par total of 142 to finish second and win £140, followed by a poor 75 in the Pro-am. With no let-up in the punishing schedule, two days later I was at the Robin Hood Golf Club Pro-am in Birmingham. This was a course I never found easy, tight and tree-lined, but on this occasion I did play it well with a five-birdie round of 70, two under par, and finished second, winning £150.

It was September now and, although I was becoming more troubled by my inability to swing smoothly, my good form continued. Some people thought I had the yips, but I didn't think so, as sometimes I was fine and other times I was very shaky, and many times I had played great golf under extreme pressure. I tried to put it to the back of my mind and concentrate on playing golf.

I did well in Pro-ams at Sandwell Park and Erewash Valley and then it was the Midland Open at Forest of Arden, which was fast becoming an excellent course. I played some fine golf, especially in the first round to score 71, 74 and finish in fourth place behind winner Brian Waites to win £171. In the subsequent Pro-am on the same course I shot 72 to be third Pro and collect another £100. It had been a good three days work.

On Friday 25th of September it was Emily's second birthday and it was also the first day of the 36 hole Midland PGA tournament at Newcastle-under-Lyme Golf Club. This was a new course to me, but I got the hang of it quickly with a fine four under par round of 68 to be one shot off the lead. I had hit 16 greens in regulation including eight times within 15 feet. The tidy round contained four birdies and 14 pars and I couldn't wait for the following day's final round. Saturday's round got started in heavy rain and before long the course became unplayable. The day's play was cancelled and the second round was unusually re-scheduled for three weeks later.

Just before the Newcastle tournament would be completed I was off again to Portugal for the final of the 3 5's Pro-am at Penina. Two years earlier I had played in the same event so I knew what to expect. Staying at the luxurious Penina Hotel with everything provided, it should be a great week. The prize-money was generous for the 54 hole tournament, but the only disappointing aspect was that it was all for the better-ball score and there was no individual Pro's competition. This would put a lot of pressure on my amateur partner, Doug Hands.

Penina, Henry Cotton's masterpiece would be a long, stern test off the back tees, not quite the championship tees but lengthy enough, nevertheless. The Sutton Coldfield team was supported by club captain Moss Dudley, invited along courtesy of the sponsors and by the time Tuesday arrived we were ready for action! I hit the ball superbly in round one, missing only one fairway and one green and getting inside 15 feet in regulation no fewer than 10 times. However, my conversion rate on the greens was disappointing and in the end I was round in a one under par 72. Doug could not find his best form and our better-ball score was also 72, just one off the lead in second place. Next day, with the wet course playing its full length, my excellent striking continued and with five birdies and one bogey I shot 69, four under par. Poor Doug couldn't get into the game and our team score was also 69. Our 36 hole total of 141 was lying third, only one behind the joint leaders. We knew a good final round could win us the tournament, but my form deserted me somewhat on the front nine and Doug still struggled to find his game. I had a nice birdie two on the 13th and an eagle three on the 17th to help salvage a better-ball 74. Doug had bettered my score once in this round and felt bad about his small contribution but really it was unfair to pile

Penina, Portugal, with Doug Hands, 1981.

such pressure on the amateurs by having all the Pro's prize money for the better-ball score. I was just grateful to have had the free trip and pleased to have played so well. Our 54 hole score of 215 was good enough for seventh place and won me a cheque for £330.

Less than a week after returning home, the concluding round of the Newcastle-under-Lyme tournament was finally played on a cold and windy day. After being in second place for the unusually long period of three weeks I played steady, if not spectacular golf to score 73 which put me in a tie for first place with first round leader Angus Dow. On a very cold and dismal October evening we set out on a sudden-death play-off. The first at Newcastle is an uphill, short par-four and after a nice drive I managed to hit a lovely 9 iron eight feet from the flag and proceeded to convert the putt for a winning birdie. My reward was £220 and subsequently I had the pleasant surprise of being informed that I had won the Midland PGA's order of merit for 1981. An excellent end to the year!

It had been a year of great progress for my game. Over 86 competitive rounds I had averaged 73.2, with nine scores in the sixties and just three in the eighties. My winnings were over £5,500, worth about £17,000 today, and I was full of confidence except for one thing. My movement control was getting worse and I was afraid it could be something dangerous. I had seen my doctor a couple of times and had tried hypnotherapy, but I knew they hadn't got to the root of the problem. In December I spoke to the Captain's son, Paul Dudley, who was a young G.P. and arranged a meeting in January to discuss the situation. My dilemma was that on the one hand I was on the brink of making a breakthrough in big-time golf and on the other hand I may have a life-threatening disease.

My shop at Sutton was barely viable, but with the retainer and green fee commission from the club and very low overheads, it provided a solid base for my tournament play. Tony, one of my assistants, had decided to leave at the end of the year and I decided to advertise for a replacement in January. Ian was still there and his grandfather Fred helped out in the shop when needed. The members were mostly supportive and proud of my achievements, but I am sure some thought I should spend more time at the club. The Club Pro faces an impossible task trying to please all his members. He is expected to win tournaments, teach like David Leadbetter, retail like Marks and Spencer, remember all the members' names while always being available in the shop for advice! Teaching was an area where I was developing a good reputation, although the poor practice facilities at Sutton made it impossible to give a large number of lessons. I had always been able to help people with their games and having played with many top players I knew what a good swing looked like.

Leaving my health worries aside, I decided to go on the Safari Tour again in the New Year. It would be a four-week trip this time taking in four big tournaments and several small Pro-ams. I would plan the rest of my season based on my performance on the 'dark continent'!

07

Shakin All Over

1982–aged 28

There were a few alliances over the winter plus the regular Sunday morning Captain/Pro matches at the club, in which pairs of members would challenge myself and the captain to four-ball matches. Towards the end of the month I visited Dr. Dudley for his opinion on my movement problems. He then referred me to local consultant neurologist Adrian Williams within a week. Professor Williams was quite fascinated by my condition, which he called dystonia. He suggested I try beta-blockers and wanted me to see a top specialist in London.

A couple of weeks later I had a request from Professor Williams to attend a medical conference in Birmingham where he wanted to show me to his colleagues and get their input about what was going on in my body. Along I went with a club and with Professor Williams' help, explained to the assembled medical experts the trouble I had. It was one of the most bizarre experiences of my life, standing on a stage in front of dozens of eminent doctors, demonstrating my shaky swing! Various ideas were put forward, similar to what I had already heard, but there was no conclusive diagnosis. An appointment was made for me to see Professor David Marsden at The Maudsley Hospital in London on April 16th, just after I was due to return from Africa. This whole business was, of course, very unsettling but both Rosie and I knew I had to be properly diagnosed.

Despite all the upset caused by the above, preparations had to be made for the Safari Tour and there was lots to do. My assistant Tony now put in his notice, mainly due, I think to his lack of progress with his game. Now being down to one assistant, Ian, helped by his grandad Fred, everything had to be in place for the shop to run smoothly in my absence. Fortunately, Rosie would be on hand to check on them and do the banking. She had stopped teaching when Emily was born and could help at the club from time to time.

On Sunday March 7th I set off on my sixth and final African Safari Tour. Following an over-night flight we arrived in Nairobi early morning, and after a coach ride to the Muthaiga Golf Club I went straight out to play with fellow Midlands Pro Charlie Ray. Sharing a room with Bill McColl, I was staying in the lovely old colonial style house of George and Pat Varney. An early start on Tuesday morning for the Pro-am suited me fine, not too hot. After a poor start, I recovered well with six birdies to score a level par 71 to finish seventeenth. Quite encouraging, but in the afternoon I had a dreadful experience. While hitting some balls on the practice ground together with some other players, I was shaking terribly. It was so embarrassing that I had to stop after 20 minutes. The beta-blockers didn't seem to have any effect. Wednesday's practice round was very similar and my confidence level was dropping alarmingly.

Next day the Kenya Open got started at Muthaiga. I started swinging more freely but had an up and down round to finish on 76, well down the field. Off at 12.50p.m. in Friday's round, it was particularly hot, and after another poor practice session I hit the ball reasonably well but could only manage 74. I would require a good third round just to make the cut. Saturday was my 29th birthday, and I always played well on my birthday! Out of a field of 88, the leading 50 players would go through to the final day, and I was in 50th place after 36 holes. Despite striking the ball fairly well in round three, I made some silly errors and found myself four over par after 10 holes.

Then suddenly I got it all together and played the last eight holes in two under par for a 73, vitally birdieing the 18th to scrape through the cut right on the mark. There was good money to be won on Sunday, but I was too tremulous to swing properly and it was only my experience and determination that limited the damage to 76. My 299 total was 45th and won £300. Then it was early to bed for a 7.40a. m. flight to Zambia in the morning.

After a horrific journey of nine hours, mostly involving queuing and form-filling, we walked into the Mufulira clubhouse at 2.30 in the afternoon. Staying with a Scottish couple very close to the course, I was hoping for a better tournament this week. Tuesday was practice day and I was again shaking badly, so badly that I wouldn't go on the practice ground with the others. Going out in the afternoon for Wednesday's Pro-am I began to swing and putt very well. I got to three under after 11 holes and then disaster struck. A six on the par-three 12th was bad enough, but to follow it with an eight on the par-five 13th was too much! To my credit I came back with birdies on 15, 16 and 17 to finish on level par 73. What a strange round!

With an afternoon start on Thursday the Mufulira Open started well for me. With improved putting, I got to one under after five holes and eventually finished on level par 73, in 18th place and four shots off the lead. The second round began very much like the first, one under par for the first six holes, but then some poor shots crept in. I decided my shoulders were opening before impact and by the last few holes things improved again. I finished on 76, to be lying 35th at the half-way point. On returning to the clubhouse I was delighted to find a letter from Rosie, full of news about what she and Emily had been doing and encouraging me to play well. Next day was one of the hottest of the whole trip. Playing with Paul Hoad and Peter Harrison, my ball-striking was only average, but my short game was sharp and with only 28 putts I was round in a one under par 72. On the par-three eighth I hit a 7 iron to two inches to very nearly hole-in-one.

Going into the final round in 28th position, 10 shots behind the leader, the potential was there to win a big prize. When playing on Safari, we were always allocated local African caddies. Usually they were fairly good, but on this morning my man Albert was nowhere to be seen. He eventually turned up 20 minutes late saying that he had had too much sleep! This contributed to a poor bogey six on the first, but then I slipped into gear. Only missing two of the remaining 17 greens in regulation I made five birdies and 12 pars to shoot a superb four under par 69. My two under par total of 290 gave me 18th place and a cheque for £637. This was very good news all round, because not only had I covered the cost of the whole trip with two events still remaining, but I had played excellent, controlled golf under pressure in a week that started with a lot of shaky trouble. This made me think that my problem was not yips but something else. For the moment all that was forgotten and I couldn't wait for the next tournament!

On Monday we travelled from Mufulira to Lusaka and after arriving at the golf club, I went straight out to play. The course was unusually dry this year, but the greens were good, normally a combination that leads to low scoring. The opening event was a two-day Pro-am with only five individual prizes for 99 pros. The chances of winning money weren't good, but I carried on where I left off in Lusaka and with four birdies on the front nine, went out in 32. Two further birdies and a single bogey gave me a four under par round of 69, which was good enough for third place and a prize of £190. An amusing spectacle in the Pro-am was the partnership of big Brian Barnes and President Kaunda. Apparently the President called Brian 'Son' and Brian called him 'Dad'!

Following a touch of sunstroke on Wednesday, the first round of the Zambia Open got started on Thursday and I had an unfortunate draw with two foreign players who hardly spoke any English. In a quiet round I didn't play at all badly, hitting 15 greens and 11 fairways, but left myself a lot of long putts and, unable to make a single birdie, finished with a 75 to be well down the field. Round two was one of those up and down games that you have as a tournament Pro from time to time. A scrappy front nine of 38 was mostly due to flat swinging and when I adjusted my swing plane on the tenth tee the transformation was immediate. A two-putt birdie on the 10th was followed by a long-putt birdie on the 12th. It was a sultry day and we then had a 20-minute delay for lightning. After resuming I had a bogey six on the 14th and got to the 16th tee two over par. There was a fancy new Range-Rover on offer for a one on the par-three hole and after choosing a 6 iron, my well struck tee shot homed in on the flag. It looked in for a moment but inevitably it missed and finished eight feet behind the hole. I knocked it in for a two and headed for the par-four 17th. After driving down the fairway, there was a loud roar from the 16th and Ian Woosnam, playing behind me, had holed in one to win the car! While over my second shot to the 17th, I couldn't help but think how lucky Ian was, but managed to concentrate enough to hit a perfect 5 iron to the elevated green which also finished in the hole for an eagle two! Funny old game! A par on the last gave me a 72 to pull me up to 39th position.

Saturday's third round turned into a disaster. I was going along reasonably at two over par with three holes to play, close to the cut mark but confident of getting through. Then on the par-three 16th after just missing for a two, I missed a two foot return putt to make a bogey four. Following a par on 17 I knew I needed a par five on the last to make the cut on 223. After two good woods I played a nice pitch that went about 20 feet past the flag and four feet into the clingy fringe. From there I left my downhill putt three feet short and proceeded to miss that crucial putt. Knowing I had missed the cut, to add insult to injury, I then missed the tap-in to make a seven! A putting collapse like that would have been impossible for me a year or two ago, but by now anything could happen, so I just tried to put it behind me.

Following my unscheduled Sunday off, we were soon en route to our final destination, Botswana. Stopping off in Johannesburg only to change planes, the contrast with other parts of Africa was amazing. It was big, clean and prosperous looking, but Gabarone was to be my home for the next week. Not having been to Botswana before, I couldn't believe the intensity of the sun when we arrived, and the temperature was up to 40 degrees centigrade. I thought to myself " How do you play golf in this?" During Tuesday's practice round with Tony Blackburn (not the DJ), it was so hot that his clubheads were coming loose due to the glue melting! Playing steadily in the pre-tournament Pro-am, I shot a one under par 71 containing five birdies and was hopeful of a decent performance in the main event.

Gabarone's Kalahari Classic got started on Thursday and although my ball striking wasn't at its best, my putting form had returned. An opening 71 put me in ninth place, four shots behind the leader. Round two carried on in a similar vein and a steady 72 put me in eighth position. This was good stuff and for the third day I found myself in the third last group drawn with David Vaughan and Ian Woosnam. I was a little nervous playing with Ian and hit some dreadful shots on the first five holes, doing well to be just two over par. Then suddenly I hit better form and holed some putts to play the remaining 13 holes in three under to finish on 71. My 214 score kept me in eighth position, five behind the leader going into the final round. Another great chance for a big cheque or even a victory! Sunday turned into a disappointing anti-climax. A poor ball striking round with shaky swinging could not be saved by putting this time and a 77 dropped me into 17th place. However, it was still a good finish and my £420 prize was not insignificant. I now couldn't wait to get home and after a tedious 15 hour journey I was re-united with Rosie and Emily.

This would turn out to have been my final and most successful African Safari Tour. With winnings of more than £1,500 it was very profitable and proved that I could compete at a high level, but my dystonia was a constant concern and I was due to see Professor Marsden in London the week after arriving home.

During my six tours of Africa between 1973 and 1982 I had played 24 tournaments and numerous Pro-ams with strong fields and had managed six top-20 finishes. I had only missed four cuts and generally had given a good account of myself. These trips were very influential in my development and undoubtedly were well worth the effort and aggravation. Playing in such varied conditions and putting on greens with strong nap had made me a better golfer. Only once had I failed to make a profit and would be forever grateful to the various generous hosts who made the tours possible.

On April 16th 1982 I had an appointment with Professor David Marsden, world-renowned at the time as the leading expert on movement disorders, at The Maudsley Hospital in London. After a long train and tube journey I arrived in plenty of time for my 11.30 a.m. appointment, carrying a golf club so that I could demonstrate my shaky swing if required. Following initial consultations with his assistants, the great man arrived with attentive minions in tow, somewhat reminiscent of "Carry on Doctor!" After consideration, he told me with no hesitation that he agreed with the earlier diagnosis of dystonia. The things that really shocked me were that he said that it was an incurable condition which would probably deteriorate over time and that he advised me to change my career. Apparently my brain doesn't like repetitive movement and instead of allowing it to happen, it sends the muscles into spasm, causing me to shake and lose power and control. Of course, golf is based on repetitive movement and after making hundreds of thousands of swings my brain was rebelling against it. I was only 29 years old and should have been looking forward to many more successful years of playing. Fortunately, it wasn't life threatening, but it certainly would affect my life. The return train journey gave me much time to ponder. Was this the end of my golf career?

Professor Marsden's advice was very hard to take, after all I had dedicated my last 13 years to becoming a successful tournament player and held a respected position as Professional at Sutton Coldfield, but this was the top man in his field telling me I should give up playing professionally. Rosie and I did much soul-searching and eventually came to the conclusion that I must continue to play as much as possible while I still could. Retrospectively, I am sure this was the right decision.

Two weeks later, after feeling very sorry for myself, I had a fantastic piece of good fortune which cheered me up. Playing in a 36-hole Midland PGA tournament at Stoke-by-Nayland Golf Club in Suffolk, I was having one of those incredibly topsy-turvy spells of play. My first round of 76 contained six bogeys, two double-bogeys, four birdies and one eagle! Throughout round two, in very windy conditions with firm ground, the same trend continued. Although I was playing fairly well, by the time I reached the 18th tee I had recorded every score between two and seven except for a six! The final hole was a 191 yard par-three over a lake and a car was on offer for the first Pro to hole in one. The flag was just over a step in the right side of the green and I planned to hit a 4 iron to pitch on the lower level of the green and run up the slope to the pin. After a long wait on the tee I hit the shot as planned straight at the flag, landing on the lower level and releasing up the slope, and knew it would finish close. Being unable to see it finish I didn't know that my ball was teetering on the lip of the hole, but when a huge roar came from the small gallery at the green I knew it must be in! I had won a red Ford Fiesta worth nearly £3,000 for one shot, incredible! I had also shot 74 to finish sixth in the tournament. It was great to ring Rosie and tell her she could have a new car. The only down-side was having to pay income tax on its value, but a new car for just £900 was great. We kept the Fiesta for a couple of years and it was very useful for Rosie.

Trying to cram in as much golf as possible while I could still play half-decently, my hectic schedule continued, while at the same time trying to run my shop and spend time with my wife and daughter. I had a new assistant starting shortly to partner Ian at the club. Ben Adams was a junior member at Sutton and a very promising player as well as being pleasant, intelligent and well spoken. He would prove to be a good choice, but wouldn't start full-time until early next year.

On May 6th I made the long trip to Great Yarmouth to play in a Pro-am and in nasty conditions shot 74 to finish 10th and win over £100. The very next day I was closer to home at Maxstoke Park for the 36-hole Warwickshire Professional Championship. Throughout the day I played superb tee to green golf, only missing three greens in regulation out of 36. I should have walked away with the title, but putting let me down. Taking 36 and 35 putts I scored 73, 72 for a one over par total of 145 to finish joint first with Phil Weaver, Ray Leach and Neil Selwyn-Smith. We were expecting sudden-death but the rules said that an 18 hole play-off was required, so we all had to return on May 30th. Rather a nuisance for me considering my fixture list, but it would be nice to get that title and trophy!

Three days later was the annual Stourbridge Pro-am. This was always a very raucous affair with hospitality tents and much noise and laughter from the enthusiastic galleries. This year I played solidly and despite poor putting, finished second with a 71 to win £200. I then suffered a few sub-standard performances in a row, which culminated in the Warwickshire Pro's Championship play-off at

Maxtoke. Out of the four of us it was expected to be between Phil Weaver and myself, but it didn't turn out that way. Neil Selwyn-Smith shot 70 to surprisingly win by three strokes and I was 75 to be third, winning just over £100 for my efforts.

June came around and I was back on form. In a Pro-am at The Belfry I shot a two under par 71 to be first individual Pro and with my team finishing third I picked up £250. On one of the most demanding courses in the country I hit 15 greens in regulation including eight times inside 15 feet. For some unknown reason The Belfry would turn out to be one of my most successful venues even though I always have found it a daunting test. The following week on another good hunting ground of mine, Staverton Park, I was again playing well. Rounds of 68 and 73 on the par 71 track put me in third place in a Midland PGA tournament, five shots behind winner Pip Elson. In the post-tournament Pro-am I shot 72 to be third and brought in the winning team. Over the three days at Staverton I had made 11 birdies and an eagle and won a very handy £370.

Another sticky patch then followed where I won very little money. It lasted until the end of July and included three big events, The Club Pro's Championship at Hill Valley, The English Classic at The Belfry and The Open. In windy conditions at Hill valley I lost the ball with my very first tee shot and despite making 11 birdies over the four rounds, I was never in control and shot 302 to finish 35th. At The Belfry for a Tour event on uncharacteristically bumpy greens I scored 81 to fail to pre-qualify. The '82 Open was at Troon and Glasgow Gailes was my qualifying course. In perfect conditions I opened with a nice 72 to be in 25th position, but on day two as the weather deteriorated so did my game and a 78 was six shots too many to get through. There would be no Open adventure this year. Various Pro-ams followed the same pattern, still making birdies but too many errors. One of these Pro-ams was at the incredibly exclusive Coombe Hill in London, where the greens were perfection.

Things got back on track at Redditch Golf Club on August 4th during the qualifying round for the Midland Pro's match-play championship. The tricky tree-lined course was running fast but I struck the ball superbly, missing just one green, to lead the qualifiers with a record-equalling, three under par 69. My first round opponent was to be Tony Minshall, my old PGA Cup partner and currently a man in form. Strangely, we both played poorly in a match where Tony was four up at the turn and after some better play by me coming back we were level again after 18. I birdied the first extra hole to win the match and would face Mike Gallagher in the second round. In the afternoon match I started off in fine fashion with birdies on the first and sixth to go two up, but Mike's putter was red hot, getting used only 26 times, and he finally won by one hole. It was disappointing to have played well and lost, but that can happen in match-play.

Our next Midland PGA order of merit tournament was a 36-holer at Patshull Park only a week later. This was a course where I always thought I could do well and after a poor start I proceeded to play some great stuff. Leaving the sixth green two over par after a mediocre start, I went on to play the remaining 30 holes in 5 under to score 72, 69 and finish runner-up, one shot behind the winner, taking home a cheque for £170. Two more course records then followed in quick succession. A fantastic day with the putter in a small Pro-am at North Worcestershire Golf Club helped me to a three under par 66, two shots clear of the field. I used only 11 putts in a back nine of 32! Five days later in a similar event at the incredibly hilly Cold Ashby in Northamptonshire I made seven birdies to set a new record of 68, two below par. This was great but I was thinking I should be doing these scores in big tournaments rather than little Pro-ams.

While all this was going on Rosie discovered that Emily would be having a new brother or sister in November. We were all thrilled, especially nearly-three-year-old Emily who would have a real baby to play with instead of her dolls!

Just five days after playing so well at Cold Ashby, we had a 36 hole Midland PGA tournament at Branston and I was one of the favourites to prevail. Feeling confident, I was about to suffer a devastating attack of dystonia, which would become an all too familiar occurrence over subsequent years. Unable to hit the ball with any authority due to tremor and weakness I did amazingly well to score an embarrassing 80 and miss the cut. Playing partner Phil Hinton must have been shocked at my play, and at that time I was not very good at explaining the dystonia to people, and would tend to go and hide after a round such as this.

Life carried on, and despite being rather shell-shocked, later that week I was teeing up in a Pro-am at Leamington. Starting on the 10th, my muscular control was much better today and after a great double-birdie start, I hardly missed a green to shoot a one under par 71. I finished fifth Pro and brought in the second best team to pick up £182. My grand plan of playing as much as possible while I was still able continued and over the next fortnight I would be competing almost every day. Next stop was Telford, a long course with big greens where I always fancied my chances. We would play the 36-hole Telford Ironmasters tournament, but unfortunately this year the prize-money was rather poor. On day one I made a fine start, two under after four holes and continued to play well to the end, but putting let me down and a one over par 73 would be the outcome. The second round went very much the same, only missing one green and getting inside 15 feet in regulation seven times, but unable to make a putt. It added up to 72 and together with my first round 73 I would finish in 10th place to win a measly £48!

The Crusader Midland All Stars Championship at Forest of Arden, a few days later, would be my final big event of the year. With a first prize of £1200 it was a great chance for me to cash in. David Davies, writing in the Birmingham Post said " Thorp is the probable favourite to take the title, not just because he is playing well, but because he is well supplied with the virtue that this course demands most of all, patience". His prediction seemed well founded as I got off to a terrific start in blustery conditions on day one. With four birdies in the first seven holes I was on top form and was a little disappointed to finish in 71, one under par. This was still good enough to be jointly in the lead, however. Playing the back nine first on the second day, I struck the ball even better, only missing two greens on this testing layout, and four birdies offset by two bogeys would give me a 70 for a 36-hole total of 141. I was in second place, two behind the unfancied Alistair Briscoe, and two ahead of third placed Peter Seal. We would play the final two rounds on the third day and I really fancied my chances of victory. Again in windy weather I started round three well and turned at the 18th in 35, one under par. Three consecutive bogeys set me back a bit, but a nice birdie on the eighth, my 17th, helped me to a 73. I found myself three shots clear of the entire field going into the final round, not a position I was used to, but I felt I could keep it going to win.

Making the ideal start in the afternoon with a birdie on the first, I was hitting fairways and greens and feeling good. A small hiccup then occurred with bogeys on four, five and seven but after a great second shot onto the par-five eighth green a birdie followed and I was back on track. A bogey four on the short ninth over the lake didn't help, but as far as I could tell, I was still in the lead despite going out in 39. Three solid pars on 10, 11 and 12 were good but I could have done without the bogey five on the 13th. Feeling the pressure, but still playing well I made a steady par three on the 14th and then a superb two-putt birdie four on the par-five 15th. The 16th at that time was a shortish par-four with a tight drive through trees and a green set into gorse bushes. A good drive into light rough left me just a 9 iron second shot to the green. I made a nice swing but sensed a flyer as soon as club struck ball. It flew to the back edge of the green and bounced into the bushes. I thought I might be able to hack it onto the green, but incredibly we couldn't even find it! I had to go back and play another ball and finished up with a double-bogey six. It was a great shock but to my credit I played the last two holes in regulation pars to shoot 77. My 291 total put me in third place behind Tony Minshall and Alan Roach, but because Alan was an amateur I took second Pro prize of £620. I finished three shots behind Tony and would ponder how I lost that ball on the 16th, just yards off the back of the green, for a long time afterwards. After all the excitement of the tournament, I had to come back again the next day to play a Pro-am. Despite the disappointment of the previous day, I played another very solid round. Starting on the 10th, I got to three under par after six holes and finished on level par 72 to be fourth Pro and win another £85.

Just 48 hours later I had another successful day at the Olton Pro-am in Birmingham. Scoring 72, I finished second Pro and also brought in the second placed team to pick up £120. Towards the month end the Midland PGA held its final order of merit event at Royal Norwich Golf Club. In very windy conditions on an unfamiliar course I did pretty well, shooting 76, 73 to finish sixth to win £130. This result clinched my second consecutive order of merit title in the

Midlands, which pleased me greatly. I played a few more events in 1982, with a couple of notable performances. At a sodden Stratford-on-Avon Golf Club on October 8th I scored 72 to finish second while captaining the winning team to collect £160. Then a week later in a Pro-am that I organised at my own club, I shot a fine 74 in gale force winds to finish runner-up and win £140. One surprising failure was in the Warwickshire match-play at Stratford, an event in which I had been champion and losing finalist in my two previous appearances. This time I lost three and two in the first round to Steve Arrowsmith, Andy's brother.

It had been a remarkable year's golf which started with my being told to change my career and ended with my finishing top Midlands professional for the second year in a row. I had won over £5,000 and a car for a hole in one. I knew I was playing on borrowed time and sooner or later this would all come to an end, but I was determined to make the most of it while it lasted. Next year's campaign was already being planned!

On November 12th at 5.20a.m. our son Christopher John arrived in the world and golf would take a back seat for a while. Luckily he had two mothers to look after him; Rosie, his real Mum and Emily, his three-year-old sister! With the family now larger, we decided that we ought to move to a bigger house on a quieter road with more garden for the kids to play in. This would be a priority in the new year.

Things were OK at Sutton. The members were supportive of my playing and tried to patronise my golf shop as much as possible. I worked hard on the shop business, always paying my suppliers on time and keeping records up to date for the accountant. The business would have never survived by itself, but with a retainer from the club and the premises provided free of charge it made a small profit. I now had Ian and Ben as assistants with Ian's grandad, Fred, also available if needed, so the shop was always manned. Teaching was the one area where I was unable to really get stuck into for two main reasons; I was often away playing making it difficult for people to make appointments at their convenience and the practice facilities at Sutton were poor. The official practice ground was a good 15 minute walk away and was full of stones just under the surface of the ground and the alternative was to hit down the first fairway which was far from ideal when golfers were playing. However the situation at the club suited me fine while I was playing so well.

08

One Last Open

1983-aged 29

The Safari Tour had been a possibility again, but with the new baby's recent arrival we decided it wouldn't be ideal. So my first outing would be a Spanish Pro-am at the end of January, in which we were due to play one round on each of the courses Sotogrande New (now Valderrama), Las Brisas and El Paraiso. My team would include two regular partners from Birmingham, Roy Moore and Geoff Adams, who had been great supporters of mine. I started well with 74 round the difficult Sotogrande to be in third place in a strong field, five shots behind leader Howard Clark. The second day began well enough at Las Brisas with a birdie on the first but a disastrous back nine of 43 gave me an 82, my worst score for a long time. My front nine at El Paraiso in the final round carried on in the same vein but a level par back nine of 36 gave the round respectability. In the end I was 12th, winning very little money, but at least I had had some practice in the sun.

On my return we put our little house on sale with a local estate agent in Aldridge and waited in vain for a buyer. It would take some time, as it turned out. From March 1st Ben started as my full-time assistant alongside Ian, so everything was in place for another extensive playing campaign. I was well aware, however, that it was a long time since I had competed regularly at the top level. I had dominated in the Midland region, but that was a far cry from the European Tour. I would try to address that over the next couple of years.

A few winter alliances kept my competitive hand in, but I was having some dystonia trouble and it was becoming increasingly obvious to observers. As well as a wobbly backswing, an annoying weakness in my left hand and arm made me lose control of the club and some awful shots would ensue. But during periods of respite, my game would be as good as ever. Paradoxically, the more I practised the worse I got, so I tried to keep practice sessions short and concentrated more on playing holes rather than repetitively hitting balls.

I had to wait until April 26th for my first event of any consequence, a Pro-am at Stockwood Park in Luton. Playing the course blind, I struck the ball well and without making any putts, shot 71 to finish ninth and won £100. A week later I was rather fortunate in a wet Pro-am at Glen Gorse in Leicester. After starting with a nice two-putt birdie four on the first, my swing became a struggle. The rain that we teed-off in got progressively heavier, never good conditions for me and about half-way through the back nine the wheels really came off and I expected to finish out of the money. However, the course became unplayable later in the day and it was decided to make the event over the first 12 holes, since everybody had played those holes. Luckily for me, I was only one over par at that stage and that put me into third place, winning £140!

In an attempt to re-join the big league I entered the Martini tournament in Manchester and was drawn at Bramhall for the pre-qualifying. In blustery, wet conditions I never really got close to getting through with a 76 to miss out by four shots. This was disappointing but I would have another chance to mix with the elite a fortnight later in the PGA Championship at Sandwich.

Stoke-by-Nayland was my next stop, the scene of my car-winning hole-in-one just 12 months earlier. It was just an 18-hole Pro-am this year and in contrast to last year, I played a very mediocre round of 75 to finish down the field. Three days later it was the 36-hole Warwickshire Pro's Championship at Walmley. Although I was one of the favourites for the title, Walmley was not one of my best venues. No matter how well I played I never seemed to manage a low score. It had been a wet Spring and conditions would be heavy, again not suitable for me. I played solidly all day, but could only make two birdies all day and scored 71, 75 to finish third, five shots behind the winner, Phil Weaver, and one worse than Pip Elson, the runner-up. My prize was £125 so it had been a worthwhile day.

After an unsuccessful Pro-am in wet conditions at Rothley Park on Sunday 22nd May, I was off to the south coast for the PGA Championship at Royal St. Georges. I was drawn on Princes Golf Club, a former Open Championship venue in 1932, when American Gene Sarazen triumphed. A great course, in the classic links style of its close neighbours Royal St. Georges and Royal Cinque Ports. Following my successful Open at St. Georges two years previously, the skylarks were singing and good memories came flooding back. After a day's practice I was ready to go on Tuesday in the qualifying round. I relished being back on firm, seaside turf and in breezy conditions played a very solid round of golf, indeed. Hitting every fairway and giving myself five birdie chances inside 15 feet I shot a two under par 71 to finish leading qualifier! I moved the short distance to Royal St. Georges to begin my campaign.

With two practice days I would have adequate preparation, but my first task was to find a caddy. Without my brother, I was apprehensive. Would the bagman be any good? How much would he cost? I visited the caddy-master and was offered a tall, skinny guy with scruffy looking long blonde hair. After chatting to him for a few minutes I discovered he was a well-spoken Canadian called Duncan who normally caddies on the US Tour and had just turned up at Sandwich on spec. He wasn't asking for a fortune, so I took him on. Before we got started, I explained to him that I had this funny, shaky swing where my head wobbled, but that I was actually playing quite well. He looked a little apprehensive, probably fearing a missed cut, but turned out to be very positive and would help me through my unanticipated spell in the limelight.

Friday May 27th was day one of the Sun Alliance PGA Championship. It was a day for extra jumpers and woolly hats, cold and windy, but had stayed dry through the morning. I was off late at 2.50p.m. with two other qualifiers and the course would be a stern test with a tough par of 70. Striking the ball superbly and playing some of my best golf ever, I hit every fairway and green for the first 12 holes and with some tidy putting got to four under par. I couldn't help looking at the leader boards on the way round and remarkably, at this point I held a three shot lead on the entire, star-studded field! My caddy Duncan was getting very excited and after every drive he would go galloping down the fairway to work out the yardages before I arrived at my ball. I missed my first green of the round on the 13th, but got up and down for a par and on the par-five 14th, 'Suez', after pitching my third shot to six feet, just missed for birdie.

Then on the 15th tee, the rain that had started a few holes earlier, became very heavy. 15, 17 and 18, difficult, long par-fours under normal circumstances were now playing like par-fives. A bogey five on the 15th still left me on two under par and two shots ahead. The BBC cameras then caught up with me and Alex Hay said in his distinctive Scottish brogue "This could be the sensation of the championship". In driving rain, wind and semi-darkness, with very few remaining spectators, I could be seen on the par-three 16th playing a 6 iron safely onto the green and then narrowly missing my long birdie attempt. On the 17th I drove into the wet rough on the right and did well to make a bogey five. With one to play and still in the lead I hit a good drive down the 18th fairway, but due to the conditions, the green was out of range. I was now the centre of attention with cameras and sound-men all around me. Hitting a 3 wood second shot the wet club almost came out of my hands but somehow I poked it forward, about 20 yards short of the green. A nice pitch left me with a 15 footer for par but it stayed out and I had to settle for a 69 and a share of the lead with Seve Ballesteros and Mark James. They had played much earlier in the day and were lucky to have missed the rain. After handing in my card I was ushered into the Press Tent, somewhere completely unfamiliar to me. My memory of my conversation with the world's press is a complete blank, but I must have been fairly sensible as they were all very nice to me in their reports. David Davies, in the Birmingham Post wrote "Thorp started the round dressed like a golfer and finished looking like an Arctic explorer". So there I was at the top of the leader-board in the tour's biggest event. It was a surreal experience, and I couldn't wait for round two!

Saturday dawned not much improved from Friday, cold, wet and windy. Everyone was full of congratulations and on the practice ground Alex Hay came to watch me warming up and asked me a few details so as to have more to say than just "Young David Thorp from Sutton Coldfield." My playing partners David Edwards and Brian Lewis were also enjoying the attention and had been very encouraging in that opening round. The second round got underway for us at 10.50a.m. and a steady start of four straight pars kept me on the leader-board. Bogeys on the fifth and sixth were followed by a birdie on the seventh. A par on the eighth and a bogey on the ninth put me out in a respectable 37. I then struggled on the back nine but made a great long-putt birdie three on the difficult 17th, only to spoil it all with a double-bogey on 18. My 77, although disappointing, still put me in 21st place, only six shots off the lead.

The third round was again played in cool and windy conditions, but no rain this time. I had a fantastic day with my driver, hitting every fairway. Going out I couldn't hole anything and took 39 to the turn, but coming back I hit some great shots and made some putts to birdie the 10th, 16th and 17th and returned in 35 for a 74. I was now 37th and 13 shots behind the leader. In the final round, on a much warmer but still windy day, the chance was there to win a lot of money, but it all went wrong in the first six holes. Going out in 42 was very disappointing, but to my great credit I had a good back nine of 36 to shoot 78. My total of 298 was 50th, 20 shots behind winner Ballesteros, and my prize was £370. It had been a memorable week but not a profitable one. Having stayed away for eight days, I may have just broken even, but I had shown what I could do on the big stage for a short spell at least.

Back at the club there was always lots to do after being away for a while, but my television appearance at the PGA had caused quite a stir, especially since I had been featured in the evening highlights show on the first day. It was great to get back to see the family also and fortunately Rosie had videoed my TV coverage. The following Sunday I played in the Moor Hall Pro-am and after a shaky start, had a great back nine of 33 for a 72. This gave me third place and a small cheque.

Three days later and I was on the road again. This time to Manchester for the Club Pro's Championship at the unlikely venue of Heaton Park Municipal Golf Course. It turned out to be a pleasant, if short course which I enjoyed playing. I had always done well in the Cub Pro's, and after my recent exploits I really thought I would challenge for the title. It didn't quite happen though, mainly due to poor putting. I gave myself plenty of birdie opportunities; 28 times inside 15 feet in regulation in 72 holes, but could only manage eight birdies in all. My scores were 72, 71, 69, 71 for a total of 283, which on the easy par 70 layout was only good enough for 25th place and a prize of £120.

Bad putting continued to plague me in the next event, the Midland Pro's Championship and Pro-am at one of my favourite courses, Staverton Park. In very windy and dry conditions I took 37 putts in both rounds of the tournament to score 75, 76 to come in 12th. In the Pro-am with some excellent ball striking I shot a level par 71 to finish 8th. My putting total of 34 was again too high. I was getting increasingly shaky with the putter, but dare not change my method since sometimes it worked well.

We then went on the first of several family holidays to Tenby in south Wales. Our friends Richard and Susanne Mobberley and young son Matthew joined us at the Kinloch Court Hotel, adjoining the old links of Tenby Golf Club. The kids had a fantastic time on the beach and we had a great week. I am not sure if I took my clubs on this trip, but on subsequent trips I would have some enjoyable rounds at Tenby.

Back to business and the Walmley Pro-am would be my next appearance. After going two over for the first four holes I played some fine golf, covering the remaining holes in two under par for a 70 to finish fifth. Following an unusual tournament-free week I would then have an intensive fortnight of play, which would include a Tour event and the Open Championship.

Before the big tournaments there was a Pro-am at the Worcestershire Golf Club in Malvern. It was a very hot Sunday in early July and when I arrived for my 2.20 starting time the garden party atmosphere was in full swing. Sometimes it was hard to concentrate on your game at events like this, play was inevitably very slow and it was easy to lose the plot! I was well used to this, however, and was fully focused on this day. I played superbly all the way round, only missing one green and 13 times having birdie chances inside 15 feet. With adequate putting I made five birdies and 12 pars in the first 17 holes and then spoiled the round slightly by missing a short par putt on the last green. It didn't matter though, because my 67 was the day's best score and I picked up the fine first prize of £500.

After getting home late that night it was a very early start the next morning for my 8.18 starting time at the Belfry for the pre-qualifying round of the State Express Classic. The hot weather continued and so did my good play with a steady 74 which got me into the tournament with two shots to spare. There were big crowds for this event and a strong field, as it was the week before The Open, and I had plenty of local support. In the first round I was going along nicely and after making five birdies, got to the 18th tee level par. One of the most difficult finishing holes in British golf found me out this time and a double-bogey six would give me a 74. I couldn't afford many slips on day two if I was to complete the tournament, but I was to have a shaky day with the putter. With no birdies, a 79 put me out of the tournament, very disappointing on my home turf.

At least I would now have a couple of days to get ready for the Open Qualifying at Hillside and then hopefully The Open itself at Birkdale. I had been unhappy with my iron shots lately and arranged to see my old boss Bill Miller at Fairhaven for a check-up. He told me I was too close to the ball and that my grip was too weak as well as my grip pressure being too light. Putting the changes into effect, my striking improved immediately, I was now hitting a solid draw, which would prove effective at Hillside. With my 20 year old brother Andrew carrying the bag and basing myself at my mother's house in Lytham I was hopeful of another Open success.

Hillside is a tough links course running alongside its more illustrious Southport neighbour Royal Birkdale. Rated by many as a better test than Birkdale, when the wind blows off the Irish Sea low scoring becomes a near impossibility. The Open had grown and grown since I first qualified in 1976 and in the field of 125 for the 36 holes qualifying at Hillside were many famous names such as Howard Clark, Mark McNulty, Vicente Fernandez, Simon Hobday, Eddie Polland, Tommy Horton, Peter Fowler, Bill Longmuir, Mike Miller, Malcolm Gregson and John Garner. All of whom had won big tournaments. With three other qualifying courses the number of available places was small, about 12.

For the first round on Sunday July 10th, it was a lovely hot summer day. I practised well with Andrew fielding the balls and went to the first tee for my 12.20 starting time. My playing partners were Richard Masters from Yorkshire and Mancunian Noel Hunt, a talented player who would go on to become a superb trick-shot artist. Hillside's opening tee shot is rather nerve-wracking with the out of bounds fence tight on the left, guarding the railway line which is disconcertingly close. Fortunately, none of that bothered me and a nice 1 iron down the fairway left me a short iron to the green. A solid shot left me a good birdie chance, which I narrowly missed, but it was nice to get away with such a sound start. Three more pars followed, then on the 504 yard par-five fifth, following a perfect, long drive I hit a mid-iron second shot close to the flag and rolled in the putt for an eagle three! On the tricky par-four sixth, after hitting the green in two, I holed the long birdie putt. Three under par after six holes and things were looking good. Pars followed on seven, eight and nine and I was out in 33. The par-three 10th is a mere 147 yards, but played into a plateau green surrounded by bunkers and fir trees the club has to be right and mine was one too many, sending the ball over the back. Failing to get down in two, it was to be a bogey four. Back to two under. Narrowly missing a short birdie putt on 11, another birdie would follow on the par-four 12th, following a fine approach shot. Four solid pars on the tricky next few holes put me on the 17th tee at three under par. An excellent par-five sweeping uphill through a valley in the sandhills, the 17th is a memorable hole and after two shots to the edge of the green, I chipped up close and knocked it in for another birdie. 18 is a long par-four of 440 yards and with my second shot just off the green-side, I managed to get down in two for a par. It was a fantastic four under par 68 which, as it turned out, gave me a two stroke lead on the entire field. Press interviews followed and it seemed likely I would be playing in my fourth Open. However, I was experienced enough to know that the job was not yet done. With such a strong field and so few places, four or five bogeys in the second round would eliminate me.

Monday was again sweltering and I was grateful to be off early at 8.50. A good start would be important and despite missing the first three greens I salvaged two pars and a bogey. A nice par at the short fourth was followed by a welcome birdie four at the fifth. Three regulation pars and a chip and putt par at the ninth put me out in 36, right on course to qualify. Pleased to hit it close on the short 10th, I just failed for my birdie and then, out of the blue, holed a long birdie putt on the par-five 11th. Now five under par overall, surely I could cruise in safely. Golf is rarely that easy and, inexplicably, I hit a series of bad shots and putts to make four bogeys in a row. Trying hard to think rationally, I told myself that I was still one under par with three holes to play and, based on yesterday's scores, level par or one over would qualify. The 16th was a tough par-three of 230 yards and I was pleased to hit a long iron onto the green and two-putt for a three. A regulation par five on 17 put me on the final tee needing a par four for 75. My second shot ran off the side of the green leaving a tricky chip, but I was up to the task and got down in two for my par. 75 it was, to go with my 68, making a one under par total of 143. Would it be good enough? There were lots of good players out there. I would have to wait all day to find out. In the end I needn't have worried, because 147 was the mark and I would be third qualifier, with the bonus of a £100 prize.

Delighted for my brother as well as myself, we would experience the excitement of the world's most prestigious tournament from inside the ropes for a fourth time. The tented village, the grandstands, the prize-money, the TV coverage, in fact everything had grown amazingly since I first played at Birkdale in The Open seven years earlier. I loved how respectful everyone was to me. Even though I was just an English Club Pro and not a major-winning millionaire superstar I was treated the same. I knew that for this week I was seen as one of the top 150 players in the world and that was a great feeling. One thing I always found a hassle was signing autographs. It only ever happened to me at The Open and it made me realise how much patience people like Jack Nicklaus and Greg Norman must have when they are constantly being asked to sign. It did make me feel famous though, even if the autograph hunters probably had no idea who I was!

Birkdale was set up for low scoring with fairly fast running fairways and greens that were unusually lush this year. I thought they were superb, but there was some criticism of their being too heavily watered. Thick rough would catch wayward shots, however, so it was no pushover. The 112th Open Golf Championship got started for me at 8.00a.m. on Thursday morning in the company of Glenn Ralph and Nick Job, both good English players. I opened with a bogey five on the difficult long par -four first, but hit back straight away by holing a 20-footer for a birdie on the 423 yard second. Two bogeys and five pars would put me out in a steady 36. A nice par on the sharp dog-leg 10th was followed by bogeys on 11 and 12. The rest of the round would turn out to be a roller-coaster ride of ups and downs. A superb two-putt birdie four on the 13th was followed by a bogey four on the 14th. A nice birdie four on the 542 yard 15th led to a bogey five on 16. Then on the 526 yard par-five 17th which snakes its way through huge sand dunes, a good drive was followed by a perfect long iron onto the green, which in turn was followed by a successful long putt for an eagle three. Just two over par standing on the 18th tee, I missed the fairway right in a bush and after taking a penalty drop, made a double bogey six. It all added up to 75, which was not too bad, but put me in 101st position. I would need something better if I was to get into the top 80 players to make tomorrow's cut.

My second round didn't start till 12.50 so there would be lots of practice time to get things right. Practising at The Open could be a stressful experience as you were always being watched and if you weren't hitting it well there would inevitably be the odd sarcastic comment from the gallery. With my added complication of being shaky and wobbly it sometimes put me off going on the range. Also if a great striker of the ball turned up next to you it could be intimidating. I remember practising side by side with Greg Norman once and after a while I just had to stop. His contact was so crisp and powerful that the ball fizzed through the air. But conversely, I practised next to Tom Kite at Birkdale and my striking was just as good as his, if not better. The putting green was very much the same. Because of a shortage of holes on the practice green at Lytham, at a previous Open, I once found myself putting to the same hole as Jack Nicklaus, trying hard to ensure that my ball didn't collide with his!

Friday's round was again played in beautiful hot weather and scoring opportunities were there for the taking. When we arrived at the course one of the first things we saw was that my old Lancashire mate Denis Durnian had played the front nine in an incredible 28, a new Open record. I knew I would have to go low and a good start would be essential. It didn't happen, though, and it was another bogey five on the first. Pars followed on two and three and then a superb 2 iron to six feet on the 206 yard fourth led to a welcome birdie two. My putting stroke was working particularly well today, but as often happens in this silly game, I started missing fairways and greens. I salvaged one-putt pars on the fifth and sixth, but bogeyed seven and eight. Birkdale can be a very unforgiving course and if your swing goes awry it will quickly find you out. However, I was determined not to make an early exit from this Open and began to pull things together again on the tough 410 yard ninth. An ideal drive was followed by a perfect short iron to 10 feet. The birdie putt failed to drop, but I was out in 36 and still in with a chance of the cut.

A single-putt par on the 10th and a regulation par on 11 kept me in the picture, but the bogey four on the short 12th I could have done without. The 184 yard 12th at Birkdale is a hole that had caused me trouble in the past. It is played over a dip to a raised green surrounded by steep, rough-covered sandhills and protected by deep pot-bunkers. Being at the closest point of the course to the sea, it is very exposed to the wind making clubbing difficult. At least I was now past the 12th and the three remaining par-fives would provide birdie chances. The first of them was the 13th and after two wood shots, I was able to pitch and putt for a vital birdie. A par on the short 14th was followed by another birdie on the tricky par-five 15th; things were looking good! Hitting the fairway and then the green on the 16th brought another par and now it was the 17th, the par-five that I had eagled the previous day. I successfully hit my drive between the towering sand dunes and, just like yesterday, hit a great long iron onto the green. Two putts later and I was back to level par for the round. The 18th was a very testing 473 yard par-four played from a new tee on the right this year making it a dog-leg to the right. Deep bunkers lurk all the way to the green making par a fine achievement! After hitting the fairway off the tee, I pulled my second shot left of the green. Playing the 18th in the Open is always a daunting experience with thousands of spectators studying your every move from the vast grandstands, but I was fully focused on the job and played a superb chip close to the flag. Knowing I probably needed the six foot putt to qualify I knocked it in for a 71. My 36-hole total of 146 just got through and I would be one of 83 players in round three of The Open!

Absolutely delighted, Andrew and I went to sort our stuff out at my car in the car-park. There were thousands of cars but nobody about as everyone was watching the golf. As we were chatting a familiar looking figure was walking towards us. As he got closer we realised it was the great Jack Nicklaus and he was coming to the car adjacent to ours. Jack said "Hi" in his surprisingly high voice and he and I exchanged a few words, but my brother Andrew was tongue-tied, completely transfixed in the company of the world's top golfer! I am sure there were dozens of things he wanted to say, but nothing would come out!

The next exciting thing would be to phone home and tell Rosie I was through the cut. She must have wanted to be there, but with two young children to look after, she was following it on TV. At the end of the day the draw for round three would be made and we were keen to see who I was drawn with, as there were some big names on my score including Arnold Palmer, Tom Weiskopf, Greg Norman and Tony Jacklin. My partner for Saturday was to be American Tour player Gary Koch. A little disappointing, but playing with one of the superstars could have made me somewhat overawed.

Since both Gary and I had only just made the cut, we had an early starting time, 8.30, to be precise, in the third match of the day. In front of us was the legendary Arnold Palmer and playing behind us would be Tom Weiskopf and Greg Norman. In that kind of company I did not want to embarrass myself and was trying to be positive. Palmer, playing with Gordon Brand galloped ahead of us at a brisk pace and we didn't see much of them. At the age of 53, Arnie would go round in a remarkable 68 today and would attract much TV coverage, much to the annoyance of my three-year old daughter Emily who apparently kept saying "Arnold Palmer again" while hoping in vain to catch a glimpse of her Daddy and Uncle Andrew!

It was a warm and breezy Saturday and it started badly for me, driving in the rough at the first and taking a double-bogey six. With a quarter of the field to be eliminated in today's cut, I knew I would need some great golf from here on to make the final day. I then had a spell of good play, hitting six greens in a row and two-putting every one for par. On the eighth I made a fine par four after driving in the rough and following a nice drive down the ninth, hit an iron onto the green only to three-putt for a bogey five. This was my first three-putt for 45 holes and it seemed to unsettle me. My nine-hole score of 37 was not bad, but I would need to break par coming back to have any chance. My playing partner Gary Koch was going along very well, hitting a 3 wood down the middle off most tees and following some fine iron shots with aggressive putting. He was beginning to attract quite a gallery as we made the turn.

Behind us Weiskopf and Norman were having a long driving contest, both booming monster drives on every hole and I was aware that we seemed to be holding them up. I drove into a fairway bunker on the 10th, making a bogey five and things began slipping away. On the par-four 11th I hit my second shot right of the green and found my ball in a deep rut in the ground, just five yards or so from the green. It wasn't marked as GUR, but I knew it should be and called Gary over to take a look. He said that I should get a ruling, so we called for a referee. In the meantime, back down the fairway Tom and Greg were impatiently waiting to play their second shots. We decided to wave them through and it was a relief to not hold them up any more! I was granted my free drop but failed to get down in two and it was another shot dropped. Now five over par for the round, my chances were all but gone. My main concern now was to play respectably and not distract Gary, whose round was turning into a low one. I managed that except for one embarrassment on the par-five 13th. After waiting for the green to clear before hitting my second shot, I made the most awful, uncontrolled swing with my 3 wood and sliced the ball way over the gallery's head and into uncharted undergrowth. Not wanting to delay proceedings, I dropped another ball, declaring the first one lost and hit it onto the green. A poor back nine of 43 gave me an 80, the highest score of the day, which was very disappointing. My winnings were £400 to go with my £100 from the qualifying, not much compared to current prize-money, but I was pleased with it.

Gary Koch shot 66, the lowest score of the day and went on to finish 14th on Sunday. Greg Norman also did well with a 70 and would eventually be 19th. Tom Weiskopf shot a 69 and finished up 45th and Arnold Palmer was finally placed 56th. The winner was, of course, Tom Watson who hit a fantastic 2 iron into the last green to take the title by one shot from Hale Irwin and Andy Bean. Retrospectively, mine was a fine performance. It was my fourth and last Open. The field was incredibly strong and I could be proud of making the first cut. I had, in fact, made the 36-hole cut in all my four Opens and once, at Sandwich, had played all four rounds. This was certainly one of my finest achievements in golf and, subsequently, The Open has always been a special occasion for me. It was also pleasing that my brother, Andrew was able to caddy in all of my Opens. We always made a good team.

After being away for a week and a half, it was great to go back home to Rosie and the kids. They had followed my progress closely and would have loved to be there in person, but the children were just too young. There was plenty to do back at the shop and many congratulations from the members on my return. I would usually follow success in a big event with a run of good form in lesser tournaments, and this period would follow that pattern.

A week after the excitement of The Open, I played in the State Express Pro-am at the Belfry. This was the same national Pro-am area final that I had won twice previously at the same venue. Hitting the ball very well, I made five birdies, no mean feat on the Belfry and we finished third with a better-ball score of 68, winning me £100. A notable thing about this round was that I drove the famous 10th green, not from the forward tee placed for the Ryder Cup, but from the front of the back tee with a 3 wood. There must have been a strong following wind!

Then on to the 36-hole Hill Valley Pro-am at Whitchurch in Shropshire and in warm but windy conditions I would play very steadily throughout. My level par first round of 72 put me in second place. Only missing two fairways off the tee, I missed six greens in regulation, but five single putts and no three-putts saved my score. In round two I hit the ball much better into the greens, but the putter began misbehaving. It was, however, a 71 and my one under par total of 143 gave me fourth place, five shots behind the winner, and a cheque for £255. After a late finish in Whitchurch and about four hours sleep, it was an early morning drive to Swindon for another Pro-am. Playing the course for the first time, I made a fantastic start, and with four birdies on the front half, I went out in a three under par 32. Striking it solidly on the back nine but unable to hole a putt, I returned in 38 for a one under par 70 to finish second, just one off the lead, and pick up another £200. This was proving to be a good week!

It wasn't finished yet though, because on Sunday, back at my club, I had a truly remarkable round. I had shot many low scores at Sutton in the past, but this would surpass all of them. Playing in one of our regular Captain/Pro games, where the Captain and I take on challengers in fourball matches, I was playing with the captain of the day, Ron Wright. My form was good from the start and with birdie opportunities on every hole, I could tell something special was happening. Four birdies on the front nine was good, but I had done it before, and then after birdies on the 10th and 12th, things began to heat up. Par on 13 was followed by an eagle three on the 14th and I was eight under par! Mere pars on 15 and 16 and then a big birdie, birdie finish on 17 and 18 would bring me home in 29 for an unbelievable 62, 10 under par, containing eight birdies, an eagle and nine pars! Nobody at the club could remember a lower round, and the captain signed my card as the unofficial course record. Unofficial, of course, because it had been match-play.

As we moved into August, my only event the next week was the Blankney Pro-am. It proved to be another steady round, a 71 which put me fourth to pick up £100. A week later I played in the 36-hole

Midland PGA tournament at Branston and with a late time like 2.40 in a big field, you might expect a slow round, but this was ridiculous. It took us five and a half hours to get round which made my score even more pleasing. With seven birdies I shot a three under par 70 to open up a two stroke lead on the field. The second round began well enough but eventually the hard ground and bad greens took their toll and I added a 75 to my 70 to finish runner-up to the late David Dunk, two shots off the pace. David, a fellow Yorkshireman, was a fine player and a nice man, our paths often crossing over the years, who sadly succumbed to motor-neurone disease recently.

On Sunday the 14th there was yet another Pro-am, this time at Woodlands in Northants. On a very hot day and having to putt on terrible greens, I played well, particularly on the back nine, where I scored a three under par 32. My total of 70 was good enough for third place and another handy cheque for £140.

In the final week of August 1983 I was to play some outstanding golf, unfortunate only that it wasn't in bigger tournament. The Telford Ironmasters at Telford Hotel was always an event I relished. The course, with its large and very quick greens, seemed to suit me and considering the form I was in, my hopes of victory this year were high. The weather was hot and breezy and with the course running fast, low scoring would be possible. Round one went well and a nice birdie three on the 18th gave me a two under par 70. This put me one off the lead, which was shared by no less than five players. Round two was made up of solid ball-striking, just a few too many putts and an unfortunate six on the par-five 17th. It was a one under par 71 which, together with the 70, put me in third place, three shots behind winner Tony Minshall. Winning a meagre £130, I still had to make another trip to Telford the next day for the Pro-am.

Always a bit of an anti-climax for we Pros, the post-tournament Pro-am had to be done, and this was no exception. Feeling confident and relaxed, I set out to attack the course. I had been working on playing with a weaker grip this week and I was hitting the ball long and straight, with a touch of fade if anything. Strangely enough, this swing thought rarely worked for me before or since, but it certainly did at Telford that day. I started with a long drive down the middle and a wedge to 30 feet, followed by two putts. On the par-five second hole, my 2 iron second shot finished on the green, 45 feet away. Down in two for a birdie and on to the third. A long birdie attempt narrowly missed and it was a par. Then things started to happen; wedge approaches into the fourth and fifth both finished within 20 feet and both were holed for birdies. A superb 3 wood second shot to the par-five sixth came to rest on the green, 45 feet from the hole and two putts would produce another birdie. On the short seventh a nice 6 iron to 25 feet was converted for another birdie. The dog-leg eighth was the only green I missed all day, over-shooting with an 8 iron, but after chipping to eight feet, I holed the putt for my par four. The ninth is an uphill par 4 which normally plays quite long to a wickedly sloping green, but today I just took the drive straight over the right hand fairway bunker, hit a 9 iron to 15 feet and holed the putt! To be out in 30, six under par, was amazing.

I thought there could be some low scores today, so I decided there would be no playing safe and 'attack' would be my strategy for the back nine. After a good wedge approach to the par-four 10th, my 15 footer lipped out for birdie. On the short 11th a fine 7 iron to 25 feet was converted for birdie, then on 12 a wedge second shot to 15 feet was also followed with a successful birdie putt. I was now an unbelievable eight under for 12 holes! The par-five 13th was in range for two shots and with a 2 iron in my hands for the approach shot another birdie looked likely, but I pulled it left and had to chip over a bunker. A nice pitch to 15 feet gave me a chance, but it missed. A good par on the tricky 14th took me to the teasing, short par-four 15th. With no hesitation I launched a drive just short of the green, chipped to 12 feet and holed the putt for my 9th birdie of the round! On the short 16th another good iron shot found the green and two putts brought a par. The par-five 17th was nicely played with a 3 iron, 3 wood, wedge to five feet and another holed birdie putt. Ten under with one to go, I was getting nervous but somehow kept it going. The 18th was a 396 yard uphill par-four with out of bounds left and although I caught the drive a little thin, it scampered well up the middle and left me with an 8 iron to the green, and a solid iron shot put me 15 feet right of the hole. A little jittery by now, I coaxed the putt to the hole and it came to rest teetering on the lip. Tapping it in gave me a remarkable 10 under par 62 and victory by five shots. It also beat the previous course record by five, which had been set only the day before by my old pal Paul Hinton. My reward was £225 and the round attracted national publicity in newspapers and golf magazines. I was quoted as saying "Yes, I could easily have broken 60", which sounds rather flippant, but I suppose is true! It was widely thought that this was the lowest round ever recorded in a Midland PGA event, but it was discovered that Ryder Cup player Ralph Moffitt had shot an 11 under par 61 in the Midland Open at Blackwell in 1961. I was on a real high now and couldn't wait to play some more!

Two days later I was at a windy Chevin Golf Club in Derbyshire for a Pro-am. Playing the very hilly course for the first time, I did well for a level par 69 to finish third and pick up another £120. The windy weather continued into the next week and on Friday September 2nd we played the Warwickshire Open at an incredibly blustery Nuneaton. Opening with a birdie on the first, just standing up was a real challenge and I battled round in 74 to find myself third at the halfway stage, one shot off the pace set by Pip Elson and one ahead of Phil Weaver. The wind strengthened in the afternoon making golf close to impossible, but I got round in 76 and found myself tied for top spot with Phil Weaver. In a subsequent sudden-death play-off Phil prevailed at the fourth extra hole. I went home very tired, but £190 richer!

The following Tuesday was the 72-hole TNT Overnite Midland All-Stars Championship at Purley Chase, near Nuneaton. This was the tournament I had so nearly won last year at Forest of Arden and again I was starting one of the hot favourites. Purley Chase was a fairly new, immature course, typical of the type we usually found ourselves playing in Midland events. On a breezy opening day I made the ideal start, birdieing the first two holes. With a chip-in birdie three at the 14th and every other hole in par, I was round in 68 for a clear lead of three shots. In the press I was praised for my round; the Express and Star said "Thorp was the only player to truly conquer the awkward bounces and difficult greens of the new course. Still brimming with confidence after his 62 in the Telford Ironmasters Pro-am, Thorp earned himself a three stroke lead with

COMPETITION PRO-Am

Maurice McDowling **WHITE BOXES** 62

Competitor's No.

PGA MIDLAND REGION

| | | Handicaps | Strokes |

Player A	27. DAVID THORP		A	
Player B		Date 26/8/83	B	

Marker	Hole	Length yds.	Par	Stroke Index	Gross Score A	B	Won + Half o Lost - PTS.	Marker	Hole	Length yds.	Par	Stroke Index	Gross Score A	B	Won + Half o Lost - PTS.
	1	400	4	10	4				10	397	4	14	4		
	2	491	5	1	4				11	154	3	18	2		
	3	193	3	16	3				12	388	4	9	3		
	4	379	4	13	3				13	504	5	6	5		
	5	406	4	7	3				14	437	4	3	4		
	6	511	5	5	4				15	335	4	11	3		
	7	190	3	17	2				16	186	3	15	3		
	8	367	4	12	4				17	529	5	2	4		
	9	428	4	4	3				18	396	4	8	4		
	OUT	3365	36		30				IN	3326	36		32		

Markers Signature ...... J. GRAY ......

Players Signature ...... DAVID THORP ......

Total Length	6691		30	Gross	
S.S.S.	72			H'Cap	
PAR	72		62	Nett	

Course record 62 at Telford, Shropshire, 1983.

a three under par 68." My round contained only 27 putts using the Ping Anser putter that I favoured at the time.

Round two, in contrast, was not such a good putting day. I continued to hit the ball well, but 35 putts meant I could do no better than 73, which dropped me into second place, one off the lead. The final 36 holes were to be on Thursday, and the weather turned nasty, strong wind and driving rain would be our companions for the entire day. These conditions have never suited me, but I made a good effort and so nearly pulled off the victory. Only hitting nine greens in the morning round I scrambled well to score 75, which maintained my second place. Playing with Mark Mouland and David Russell in the final round, we had a fine battle. I played solid golf in awful conditions to shoot 72 for a total of 288. Mark scored 73 for 290 and David 70 for 286 to prevail. I finished a creditable second to pick up £380. A 72 in the post-tournament Pro-am meant another fine week's play for me. But the week was not yet over, and on Sunday I was at Burton-on-Trent for their Pro-am. I was in great demand for all the Pro-ams and found it hard to refuse an invitation. At Burton, that cool and windy Sunday afternoon, I set off with a birdie and after making three more birdies and an eagle where I holed a bunker shot I finished in top spot with a 69. Another £200 in the bank!

I was having an amazing spell of play which showed no signs of coming to an end, so I just tried to enjoy it while it lasted. Four days later I was in Lincolnshire for the Belton Park Pro-am. I always felt comfortable playing here with its deer roaming across the large estate in which the course is set. On another windy day with heavy showers, playing the course for the first time, I equalled the par of 71 with some steady play and again came out top Pro to win £250. What a roll I was on! Next day I was closer to home at the Walsall Pro-am. With no improvement in the weather, I made another great start, birdieing three of the first six holes to be out in 33, using a mere 12 putts. The back nine was a disappointing 38 with 17 putts and my 71 put me in third place, which, for some reason, won very little money.

The busy schedule continued with a Sunday Pro-am at Olton in Birmingham. On another windy day I again played competent golf to shoot a level par 69, taking second place and another good cheque. That evening I was on the road to Norfolk with a team from Sutton to play in a 54-hole Pro-am at Cromer, Hunstanton and Sheringham. These were all fine, old links courses, but playing them all blind would not be easy. The weather was still not kind to us, with wind every day and some rain. Throughout the event, I never really found my 'A' game, as Tiger would say these days, and scored 76, 77, 72 to finish down the field.

Later that week the sun finally came out for a Pro-am at Stratford on Friday. Striking the ball well, I made five birdies en route to a two under par 70 to finish third and win £120. The next big event was Emily's fourth birthday party on Saturday afternoon at our house. A number of her friends came to the house and together with her little brother Christopher, not yet one, they had a great time. On Sunday I was at the unlikely setting of Brandon municipal in Coventry for a Pro-am. None of us knew the course and I was amazed when I finished top of the list again with a one over par 73 to win £215!

The following day, Monday, saw me at yet another Pro-am. This time at Dudley, 'one of the finest courses of its kind', as one old Pro used to say! On a warm day I repeated my winning performance of 1979 to score a one under par 67 to take the £100 first prize. I had played consistent golf, making four birdies and three bogeys. On Sunday of the same week at the Sandwell Pro-am it was to be very much the same story. As the Express and Star put it "David Thorp's recent near-monopoly of the local Pro-am scene continued at Sandwell Park yesterday". On a breezy day I hit the ball superbly round the testing track, missing only three greens to score a one under par 70 to win by three shots and take the £125 first Pro prize.

This had been an amazing spell of play, possibly my best ever. In the 12 weeks since the Open I had won six Pro-ams and my stroke average for 33 rounds in that period was 71.1, including 19 rounds of par or better. If I could produce that form in big tournaments I would be successful. It was about this time that I decided to go to La Manga, Spain in November to attempt to gain a European Tour card for 1984. I had been a card-holder for the tour for some years, but the rules had changed and as I hadn't won enough money on the tour this year to retain my card, I would have to qualify for it at the La Manga tournament. Local journalist Dick Norman wrote an article about me in the Express and Star on Saturday October 1ˢᵗ 1983 and said "David Thorp, having flirted with big-time golf over a number of years, is to compete for his European Tour card at La Manga, Spain, in November." He went on to say how well I had played this year and that I intended to play about 12 tour events in '84. I said how generous my club had been to allow me to do this, and retrospectively, I have to be very grateful to the Sutton Coldfield members. People like Doug Bashford, Moss Dudley, Peter Saunders and Ron Wright were tremendously encouraging, and I really wasn't at the club much through the summer months.

Another useful thing was about to happen. Dick Craven-Jones, club member and owner of 452 Motors in Birmingham was giving me a sponsored car for a year. It was a sign of my growing confidence that I could drive a white Vauxhall Cavalier full of advertising, but this new found self-belief wouldn't last long as the dreaded dystonia caught up with me in the future.

Now in October it was again time for the Warwickshire PGA match-play, this year at Harborne. A narrow victory by one hole over Neil Selwyn-Smith in round one saw me up against Steve Arrowsmith in the second round. Steve was the younger brother of Andy, my former assistant and had beaten me in last year's match-play, but today he was unlucky to come up against some of my best stuff. I got through by four and three to meet Pip Elson in the semi-final. He was always a gritty competitor and when his putter was hot there was no stopping him. In an exciting up and down match, Pip prevailed three and two. I won the consolation match for third place against John Gould two and one to net £115 for my efforts.

Shortly after this I started to have a nasty spell of jittery wobbliness which hindered my progress substantially. Fortunately most of the year's events were over, but I still had the costly Tour qualifying to come and my confidence had taken a jolt. In early November I went up to Fairhaven to play nine holes with Bill Miller, who had helped me so much before the Open. He said that I had begun to get a bit flat and loose in the left hand. This was a trend that seemed to be connected to the dystonia, my left hand and arm would become weak during the swing and my plane flattened. I would then become too right side dominant and all sorts of bad shots could result. He thought my putting stroke looked as good as he had ever seen it with the Bullseye putter to which I had now changed.

On November 19th I set off to Gatwick airport to join up with the other players for our week in Spain. There was a huge field for the qualifying event, not just from Britain but from all over the world. The desire to be a tournament playing star was now global, and it would be no pushover to get a card. I had played La Manga once before, nine years ago on that ill-fated trip in 1974 when I failed to get through the pre-qualifying round for the Spanish Open. It was a superb complex in an isolated location, with two courses and a large hotel. Going out for my first practice round, I was shocked to find the greens in a dreadful state. The grass seemed to have died and the surface was mainly sand, which had been spread to try and smooth out the bumps. Apparently, sea-water had been mistakenly sprayed on the greens and it had killed the grass. Putting would be difficult and a lot of patience would be required. This was a quality I had and I knew I could cope with the frustrations the greens would inevitably provide. Playing practice rounds with familiar faces such as Phil Hinton and Richard Lane was nice, but I was really struggling with dystonia and hitting balls on the range was such a trial that I restricted my long game practice to a minimum. There were European Tour cards on offer to the leading 34 players over 72 holes and with the greens as they were, nobody could predict what score would be required.

The first round got started for me on the North course and after hitting my second shot onto the par -four first green, I three-putted for a bogey. Hitting back with a long birdie putt for a two on the second, I then hit the par-five third in two, but again three-putted on the rough surface. Bogeys on the fifth and seventh and a fine birdie two on the eighth put me out in 36. After bogeying the 10th, I proceeded to hit all remaining eight greens in regulation, making one birdie, six pars and a bogey to finish in 73, two over par. I was in 25th place and on target to qualify. A very wet Spanish morning greeted us on Wednesday, in fact so much rain had fallen that the start of play was delayed. We finally got started, on the harder South course this time and my driving was letting me down. Hitting only five out of 14 fairways, I did well to hit 12 greens in regulation out of the wet rough. I also did well on the horrendous greens, taking only 30 putts to score 73, one over par. I was now up to 18th position at the half-way stage and the greens were playing havoc with everyone's patience and scoring.

Back on the North course for round three, my driving was still poor but my iron play and short game were saving me and the round was to be another 73, which maintained my 18th place in the field. My final round would be on the South course, and all I needed was a steady performance with no disasters. Seldom have I seen so many nervous young golfers, their whole year depending on this one round. Strangely, this would turn out to be my best ball-striking round of the four, hitting 10 of 14 fairways, 14 of 18 greens, five times inside 15 feet. My putting was safe, with no three-putts, but no birdie putts would drop for me today. It turned out to be 17 pars and one bogey for a fourth straight 73. My 292 total comfortably qualified in 14th spot and a surprisingly high score of 297 was good enough for the last card. I won no prize-money for my effort and although it had been an expensive week, I was now eligible to enter most tour events in 1984. Some notable players gained their cards that week, Andrew Oldcorn being one; I played with him for the first 36 holes and he went on to finish joint first for the week on 283. Other qualifiers were Peter Mitchell, Jeremy Bennett and my friend Richard Lane from Stourbridge, who would later go on to be Pro at Moor Allerton in Leeds.

It had been a tremendous year's golf. Playing about 80 rounds, I had won around £6,000 and my stroke average was 72.8. I had briefly led the PGA Championship, I had played three rounds in The Open, I had won seven Pro-ams and with high finishes in several Midland events, I had narrowly failed to win a third consecutive Midlands order of merit. Now a fully-fledged member of the European Tour, I should be looking forward to a bumper year to come, but I knew my future playing career was in doubt. Just 18 months earlier the world's leading expert on movement disorders, Professor Marsden, had advised me to give up playing because of my advancing dystonia. I had defied him and had just had my best ever year, but how long could it last?

09

Do It While You Can

You would have thought that I would be off around the world playing all over the place, but in fact it would be four months between the tour qualifying and my next tournament, apart from winter alliances. I think this was because wherever I chose to play over that period would be expensive and I was becoming increasingly apprehensive about the effect my dystonia was having. However, it was nice to spend more time at home with Rosie and the children and to have the opportunity to organise things better at my club shop.

Another priority at that time was our moving house. After having our house on sale for a long time with an estate agent, we took it out of his hands and bravely erected our own board. Eventually we had a buyer and had now found a suitable new house with the moving day scheduled for March 9th. The transition was successfully achieved and we were soon installed at 8 Ringwood Avenue, about a mile from our first house in Aldridge. We were very pleased with our new abode, with its more spacious interior and much bigger garden for the kids to play in.

My first proper event of the year would be the Sunningdale Foursomes, partnering my former assistant and good pal Andy Arrowsmith. Andy was not as experienced as me in playing large tournaments, but was a steady player and we thought, with a bit of luck, we could win a few matches. Our first round draw could not have been much tougher; we were drawn against local hero Michael King, affectionately known as 'Queenie' and another very useful Sunningdale member. Our match attracted a sizeable gallery and, against expectations, we went ahead. In fact, we went well ahead and were on the verge of closing them out at three up with four to play, when, out of the blue, they holed a long putt on the 15th. They went on to win 16, 17 and 18 to beat us by one hole. We were gutted and even Queenie said that we should have won! Both Andy and I revelled in the Sunningdale ambience and the quality of the course makes it one of my favourite places to play golf.

I was still, tentatively, pressing ahead with my grand plan to play a dozen tour events as well as Midland and Warwickshire tournaments, but my inability to control my movement during putting and swinging was becoming increasingly troublesome. Sometimes I would be fine and all the old skill and power were there, but at other, unpredictable times I would be so shaky and weak that it was a real struggle to play at all.

My first big outing of the year would be the Tunisian Open in mid-April and a week prior to departure I went to see Bill Miller at Fairhaven for a swing check. Flying from Heathrow on Monday the 9th in the evening, we didn't arrive at our hotel until after midnight and were shocked to discover that there was to be a pre-qualifying round the following morning to reduce the number of players to the required amount. Never having seen the El Kantoui course before, Tuesday's round was more than just the expected practice run, it was a card and pencil job and if I didn't play well I wouldn't even start the Tunisian Open! Fortunately, I did perform nicely and a three over par 75 easily qualified. I enjoyed the course which had some real links-like holes running along the beach, but it was running fast and the greens were rather bumpy. I played fairly well in the opening 36 holes, but never quite got to grips with the conditions and found myself needing a birdie on the difficult par-four 18th to make the cut.

After laying up short of the lake off the tee, I hit a superb 6 iron onto the green, 15 feet from the hole. The birdie putt narrowly missed, as did the return for a par. I had scored 76, 78 and now had the week-end off and would win no money; an expensive start to my season. Just to make things worse, that evening I developed a severe tummy upset and proceeded to spend most of the next two days in bed!

On returning home I was due to play in the Northern Open in Scotland, but still didn't feel well so I withdrew to recuperate. Later in the month we had a new tournament, the Midland Club Pro's Championship at Belmont in Hereford. This original Belmont course was long and tough with huge trees and the River Wye adding to the problems, making scoring higher than usual, but with smooth greens and surprisingly hot weather, I played some steady golf. Shooting two 77's, I finished in 4th place, five shots behind winner Pip Elson and picked up £190.

Several days later I was off to Suffolk for a 36 hole Pro-am at Ipswich and Felixtowe. April had been incredibly warm and the Ipswich course was baked hard, but with very little grass cover it was almost impossible to play, and it took me 82 shots to get round. In contrast, the Felixtowe links was in excellent condition and my game suddenly came good. With five birdies and an eagle, a five under par 67 hauled me up the field from nearly bottom to fourth place to win £150. This was very pleasing, as it is all too easy in golf to give up after a bad first round. In the past most of my successes had come with fast starts and to dig deep and stage such a come-back was gratifying.

In early May I visited Martin Hall at Trentham Golf Club for a lesson. I had known Martin for some years and he was developing a reputation as a teacher, so I decided to consult him. I think I was now clutching at straws to regain control over my game. Having played well for 12 years or so, it would be unwise to change my swing now, but I was keen to try anything to extend my career. Martin was very helpful and I would see him again in the future, but there was to be no dramatic improvement. He would go on to be a top coach in America and I recently saw him giving advice on the 'Golf Channel'.

The Warwickshire PGA championship was held at Robin Hood in '84, never one of my favourite courses. I had a poor day, scoring 81, 79 to finish 18th, failing to qualify for the match-play and just getting into the Warwickshire Open. This result must have been a real surprise to everybody, but my form was becoming increasingly unpredictable. Two days later I had a good putting round in the Stourbridge Pro-am to score 72 and finish third to win £190. A couple of days after that I was back at Stoke-by-Nayland, scene of my car-winning hole-in-one in 1982 for a Pro-am. Playing solidly and putting well with the Bullseye putter, I shot a level par 72 to pick up a handy £240.

The increase in confidence gained from the previous two rounds was seriously reversed the following week in the pre-qualifying round for the PGA Championship at the testing, tree-lined Foxhills course in Surrey. After a four- hour rain delay, we got started at 5p.m. and I was in a terrible state, unable to swing or putt without shaking badly, finally carding 82. This was particularly frustrating, as only 12 months earlier I had led the qualifiers at Princes and shared top spot in the first round at St. Georges.

Exactly a week later I was back at the same venue, Foxhills, for the pre-qualifying round of the Jersey Open. It was sensibly in Surrey to save competitors the trouble of travelling to Jersey and possibly failing to qualify. Playing with New Zealander Simon Owen, who famously narrowly lost out to Jack Nicklaus in The Open at St. Andrews in 1978, I didn't know what to expect. Inexplicably, I was on top form that day, hitting 17 greens in regulation, six times inside 15 feet. With a slight change of putting grip, moving my right hand down the shaft, I also putted well. The result was a magnificent 68, five under par, which led the entire field by two shots. My play had become incredibly topsy-turvy, seemingly either scoring in the sixties or the eighties! That afternoon I was on a plane for the short flight to the beautiful island of Jersey to take my place in the tournament. I loved the La Moye course, a real old-fashioned links in great condition, but I found the greens tricky to read. Over the opening 36 holes I struck the ball soundly, hitting 28 greens in regulation, including a couple of par-fives in two, but my putting totals of 36 and 34 were too high. Scoring 75, 74 I missed the chop by three shots and limped home without reward.

After withdrawing from the following week's tour event and two poor performances in Pro-ams, my next outing would be the Club Pro's Championship at Bolton Old Links on June 11th. This had been a good tournament for me in the past and I was hoping for more consistency than of late to produce a high finish. I loved the heathland course high up on the Penines and on a very windy opening day, driving great and putting well, I shot a one over par 73 to be in 12th spot. In similar conditions on day two, my driving was again excellent, but I couldn't buy a putt and 75 was the best I could do. Lying 22nd on the third day, the wind grew even stronger and my form slipped; my disappointing 77 dropped me to 37th place. The final round was played in much calmer conditions and my ball striking improved greatly, but my putts refused to drop. A 75 put me in 40th place to win a measly £55.

Things were not good. It was now mid-June and I had not yet won £1,000 for the year. People were wondering what was wrong, but at this stage I had kept the dystonia confidential and only a few friends and relations knew. Staverton Park was a course I always played well, surely I could find some form there in the Midland Pro's Championship. In sweltering conditions, I played steadily for 14 holes to be one under par and then couldn't swing at all on the last four holes, doing well to shoot 72. In the second and final round, hitting it well all the way and putting nicely I scored a fine 68 to pull up to ninth, just four shots behind the winner, but won very little prize-money. In the post-tournament Pro-am, on a warm but windy day I played very well for 69 to take top Pro's prize and brought in the second best team score to pick up a welcome £240.

A week later we were on another of my favoured courses, Telford, for the Ironmasters tournament. On a blustery first day, I made a great start with birdies on the first two holes. Hitting it well all the way round, I was unlucky to lose a ball on the sixth and finished in 71, one under par, to put me in eighth position. For day two we had some rain to contend with, but I again started eventfully, three-putting the first for bogey and then making an eagle three on the second. With the greens not at their best, I couldn't hole a thing and my 73 put me down in 12th place. In the following day's Pro-am, thoughts of last year's 62 came flooding back as I again began with two birdies, but I couldn't maintain it and my 71 put me in sixth place, with little reward to show for it.

In early July I was at Hill Valley for their now annual 36-hole Pro-am. The course was running fast, but the greens were holding, conditions in which I normally did well. Starting with a birdie four, I hit the ball pretty well and then unluckily lost a ball on the dog-leg ninth. A level par back nine gave me a 74, putting me six behind leader John O'Leary. Starting round two on the 10th in very hot weather, I played an almost flawless nine holes of 30, with five birdies and four pars. After getting down in two from a green-side bunker on the par-five first for another birdie, I went to six under par after 10 holes and knew this was one of those special rounds. A hooked drive into trees on the third brought a bogey and standing on the seventh tee, my 16th, I was five under par. On the par-five hole, following a perfect, long drive I sent a 3 iron into the heart of the green and holed the eagle putt from 45 feet! A par on the eighth and it was onto the ninth to finish. After two nice shots I was 25 feet away and after being a little too bold with my birdie putt, I missed the return. Disappointing, but it was a great round of 66, equalling the course record, and boosting me to third place to win £450.

It was back to the big league again next for the Lawrence Batley tournament at the Belfry. For the qualifying, it was a windy day and with thick rough the course was a stern test. Hitting the ball with control, I got to one under par after four holes, but really struggled on the greens and found myself on the 17th tee at five over par. After a fine drive on the par 5 dog-leg to the right, I hit a perfect 2 iron to just six inches for a tap-in eagle three. Then on the very testing 18th I was left with a long birdie putt up the green. I thought it was in but it stopped on the front lip of the hole and I tapped in for 75, which proved to be one shot too many to qualify. This was hugely disappointing, so close to home on a course I had previously played well. My assault on the tour was not going well.

Another chance to play with the big lads would follow with the Open qualifying at Leven Links. The Open itself was to be at St. Andrews and with my brother Andrew again on the bag I was looking for a fifth appearance in the championship. We would be staying in luxury for the qualifying, at the Old Course Hotel overlooking the home of golf! Frank Sheridan, a member of Sutton Coldfield was the manager of the hotel and, incredibly kindly, had arranged a room for us and then a flat for our use, adjacent to the 18th green, for the duration of the Open. I played a practice round with John Hawksworth, formerly a junior member of Fairhaven together with my brother, when I was Assistant Pro there. John was now a fine player and would go on to play in the 1985 Walker Cup, subsequently turning pro. We were all surprised at the poor state of Leven; it was a nice links course, but the fairways were poor and the greens at best fair. There was no rough to speak of and low scoring looked likely.

We got started on Sunday afternoon and I made a poor opening with bogeys on the first and fourth. A nice two on the short fifth steadied the ship, but three putts on the sixth and ninth put me out in 37, three over par. A superb back nine followed with four birdies, only spoiled by another three-putt bogey on the 15th. My level par 71 put me in a surprising 40th position. Day two was another calm one, so I would have to go low. My long game was first-rate today, but I was unlucky on the greens. Only missing three greens in regulation, I had nine birdie chances from inside 15 feet and only converted twice. My only bogey was on the 14th when, after driving right down the middle, my ball finished in a deep divot hole. Scoring 70 to go with my 71 on the first day was a good effort, but I was three shots too many to qualify in this company. Rather dejectedly, I went home, leaving Andrew in the flat for the week to watch the action.

The day after Seve was punching the air in triumph on the 18th green at St. Andrews, I was somewhat unenthusiastic about playing in a Pro-am at Mickleover, a shortish course in Derby adjacent to the busy A38. I started well enough with a nice drive and a chip to 15 feet, just missing for birdie. Then on the long par-three second I hit a perfect 1 iron to three feet and tapped in for birdie, followed on the third by a sand wedge second shot to three feet for another birdie. I began to take notice, thinking that this could turn into something special. Birdie attempts narrowly failed on the next three holes, then I made two more birdies from close range on seven and eight. Par on the ninth and I was out in 30. Two more birdies on 10 and 11 put me six under par, and I was starting to get excited. Going through the back of the 12th, I chipped back to four feet and agonisingly lipped out. The 13th was another long par-three requiring a 1 iron and after hitting a great shot to 15 feet, my putt just missed. Great excitement followed on the short par-four 14th where I hit a 2 iron onto the green and lipped out for an eagle from 20 feet, but made the birdie. Back to six under with four to play, but there were no more heroics, just four pars to finish. I had done 63, six under par to win by three shots and equalled the course record. I didn't realise until later that Ian Woosnam, David Russell and Martin Poxon were in the field, which made my victory seem more impressive. My winner's cheque was a handy £250.

At the end of July, Rosie and I again took the children to Tenby to stay at the Kinloch Court, run by welcoming hosts Audrey and Rob Wilkins. We all had a great time; Emily was now almost five and Christopher nearly two and having the superb beach just a short walk away was ideal. I had to come back for a day, half-way through to play in the 36-hole Second-City Pro-am at Sutton. Playing fairly well, I helped my team to seventh place, which won £150, and drove back to Tenby early the next morning, arriving just in time for breakfast.

Soon after returning home it was again time for the Branston Midland PGA tournament. In breezy conditions I hit the ball superbly on day one, but with awful greens to putt on, could score no better than level par 73. Starting the second and final round in 14th place, again I had a good ball-striking round, missing only three greens, but this time my putting was more successful and with five birdies, I shot a fine 70. My 143 total brought me in fifth, four shots behind the winner, and netted £100.

I felt I was now playing better again, but I was about to have problems of another sort. Ian, one of my assistants who had been with me for three years was moving on, together with Fred his grandad, leaving me with just Ben. With my busy playing schedule it was vital that I found a quick replacement and fortunately, the ideal candidate turned up. Lee Bashford, son of club captain Doug, was keen to start and turned out very well, becoming a fine player and qualified professional. These days Lee is the well-respected Professional at Handsworth Golf Club and we remain good friends.

By now I had changed my plans for the year. Instead of entering European Tour events with the hope of qualifying, making the cut and finishing in the money, I had decided to concentrate on Midland tournaments and Pro-ams. The reasons for this lowering of expectations were firstly my increasingly unpredictable form due to movement control problems due to dystonia. Secondly, the tour was very expensive and time consuming whereas I could commute to Midland events from home for a fraction of the cost giving me more time to spend with the family and at the club. Thirdly, although the prize-money was much smaller in the regional tournaments, invariably I would finish in the money and make a profit. I knew it was likely that my playing career would not last much longer and I felt I had to compete at a level where I could be successful.

Several poor performances were to follow, including failing to qualify for the Midland match-play, which caused a few raised eyebrows. Then on Sunday August 26th on a perfect, hot summer afternoon I went to a Pro-am at Woodlands Golf Club in Northants. My long game was back to its best and although the greens were far from perfect, my putter was hot, getting used only 29 times. Making seven birdies, including three twos, I shot a five under par 66 to win by one shot. This was a new course record and won me £350. In his speech, home Pro Mike Gallagher was kind enough to say "Today's competition has been won by the best player in the Midlands." He meant me!

After a mediocre round in a Pro-am at Breadsall Priory, yet another Pro-am at Hill Valley typified my game at the time. On a windy day I hit two great shots onto the green at the par-five first and two-putted for a birdie. Four pars were followed by a spell where I couldn't hit the ball at all giving me a front nine of 39. Suddenly my control returned and with three birdies coming back I was home in 33 for a level par 72 to finish fourth. The following day I was off to The Herefordshire Golf Club for the first time to play in their Pro-am. Wormsley, as it is also known, is a tricky, undulating course with a number of blind shots which would make this performance even more impressive. Carrying on where I left off the day before at Hill Valley, I swung the club with great control, missing only one green and giving myself nine birdie chances inside 15 feet. With tidy putting I made four birdies and 14 pars for a 66 to win by one shot and take first prize of £350. Less than 24 hours later I was teeing off in a very different event, the Midland par-three championship at Lea Marston, near Sutton Coldfield. Making six twos over 18 holes I came in third to win £140.

About this time our little Emily was becoming 'all grown up' at the age of five and started school in Aldridge, appropriately enough, next-door to Druids Heath Golf Club. There was just no getting away from this game!

Two really poor Pro-am rounds at Robin Hood and Newcastle set me back a bit before the 72-hole Midland All-Stars at Purley Chase took place again in mid-September. I had a great record in this tournament, having been runner-up in the last two and was hoping to go one better this year. We always seemed to encounter bad weather at Purley Chase and this year would be no exception, with some heavy rain on the opening day. It didn't bother me much, however and a fine level par opening round of 71 put me in second spot, one behind Pip Elson. On a much brighter day, my ball striking was excellent in the second round, hitting 16 greens in regulation. My putting was another story, and taking 35 of them meant I would score 72 to drop to fifth place.

The final 36 holes took place on a breezy Thursday, and I got off to a flying start, playing the course the wrong way round, with birdies on the 12th and 16th, to go out in 33, two under par. Twice three-putting on the back nine spoiled things a bit, but a 71 pulled me back up to second after 54 holes. Pip, on the other hand, seemed to be playing a different tournament, and was an amazing 10 shots ahead with one round to go. In the last round I again set off very well, with birdies on the fifth and sixth and pars everywhere else, a front nine of 34 was followed by some equally fine play coming back, culminating in a fine birdie three on the 18th. To a very tight pin set on a small shelf on the back left portion of the green, I hit a full sand wedge that finished three feet away after first lipping the hole. My round of 69 gave me a one under par total of 283 to make me second by four clear shots and collect £330. However, Pip won by

11 shots to walk away with the title, making me second for the third successive year. In the Birmingham Post the following morning I was quoted as having said " I think he is slipping. I have just seen him two-putt twice!" I thought this sounded a little disrespectful, so I rang Pip to apologise and congratulate him on his performance, but what a putter he was!

Well and truly stuck on the Pro-am circuit, I missed the thrill of the big time, but it seemed best for me, so I would keep on while I could. After a couple of forgettable events my next one would be at Longcliffe Golf Club at Loughborough and my long-time friend Richard Mobberley from Bridgnorth was part of my team. This is a tough, tree-lined course on which low scoring is difficult. Despite being quite tremulous on all shots, I played remarkably well, missing only one fairway and hitting 14 greens. My level par score of 72 was good enough for joint first place and a nice cheque for £300.

Later that same week I played in another one at Llangollen Golf Club in Wales. Just about everything on the day was the opposite of what I liked. It was cold, very windy, showery, the ground was soft and the greens bumpy. With a late tee-time a slow round was inevitable; my enthusiasm for the mission was low! However, against all the odds, I started well and was two under after four holes. Struggling over the next few holes, I somehow held it reasonably together, and then hit an excellent patch of play to finish with, including birdies on the 16th and 18th. My one under par 71 finished in second place, two behind the winner, and made £170. Very pleasing in unfavourable conditions on a course I hadn't played before.

The start of October brought a very busy spell of play with six rounds in five days. It began with a big Pro-am at Scraptoft in Leicestershire with a strong field containing most of the previous year's Ryder Cup team. Opening strongly with six regulation pars, I was then inconveniently stung by a wasp on the back of my left hand. My hand suddenly swelled up and unsurprisingly I dropped three shots on the next four holes. Pulling myself back together well, I made three birdies over the closing holes to post a 71, but in that company it was only good enough for 12th place. Next day was the 36 hole Warwickshire Open at Olton. On a wet and windy day, I wasn't at my best, but my seven over par 145 was good enough for third place and £140. A few hours later and early in the morning I was playing Kidderminster in the Midland President's Trophy. David Dunk and I must have been still half-asleep because after playing the first hole, we teed-off on the 13th instead of the second. This caused headlines in the Birmingham Post "Thorp is stung by costly error", because I actually did well and had to add a two stroke penalty to my score. Making six birdies I shot 69, but had to call it 71 and finished seventh instead of joint first, winning just £70. The final leg of this marathon was the 36 hole Cold Ashby Midland tournament held over two days. With the course muddy and the greens terrible, things didn't look promising, but on the hilly par 70 track I scored 72, 69 to finish seventh. That finish didn't bring much reward, but it did put me third in the region's order of merit for the year which won an additional £250.

Just about at the end of the competitive season, there was one more big tournament to go, the PGA Four-ball Championship at Hillside and Royal Birkdale, both scenes of former glory for me. It would be a nostalgic week. My partner was Bob Larratt, a gritty competitor and fine player who consistently did well in Midland events. The weather was good for so late in the year and while Birkdale was excellent, Hillside was looking decidedly jaded. We really enjoyed playing such great courses, in contrast to the poor venues that we so often found ourselves on for Midland events. Knitting in well, but failing to find top gear, we scored 73 on Hillside and 69, 71 at Birkdale, to finish 24th. Winning £80 each, it was hardly a profitable few days, but we had some good spells of play and were pleased with our 36 holes at Birkdale.

There was one more Midland Pro-am in mid-October at Brocton Golf Club in Staffordshire and I performed well in autumnal conditions, making 4 birdies in a level par 69. Finishing third individually and bringing in the second team won £140 for me. Shortly after this was the first of two 'Pro's medals' that I organised at Sutton, where we all put an amount in the pot and played for it. On a wet and very windy day I made a great start at my home course, reaching three under par after five holes. Despite a triple-bogey seven on the 11th, I scored a level par 72, which was good enough for first place by two shots. A fortnight later, in a similar event on another wet day, I played really well for a two under par 70, but only finished fifth, due to some fine scoring by my colleagues.

Later in November, I went to Portugal for a 54-hole Pro-am at Penina, where I had played similar events before. On the long par 73 course, I started well enough with 73, but the wheels really came off in round two with an 82. 74 in the final round was better, but I finished well down the field in what turned out to be a costly week.

My playing would now be restricted to winter alliances and practice at Sutton for the next three months. It gave me time for reflection on the year's play and how best to approach 1985. 1984 would go down as one of my best seasons; the statistics speak for themselves- a scoring average of 72.5 for 67 competitive rounds, winnings in excess of £5,000, 15 rounds in the sixties, 29 rounds of par or better, three course records, third in Midland PGA order of merit. Despite these achievements, my big disappointment was the lack of success in tour events, in which I won no money at all, but spent a great deal trying. I had now, sadly, abandoned any hopes of being a big-time tournament player and would do the best I could in smaller events while my abilities were still with me.

One up-beat note to finish the year on was a spectacular round in an alliance at Stratford-on-avon just prior to Christmas. In cold conditions I made eight birdies and went round in a seven under par 65. My partner, Bob Brettell and myself scored a better-ball 47 stableford points to finish second team. The club kindly gave me a 10% rise in retainer for the new year to take it to just under £5,000. Assistants Ben and Lee were doing well and everything was in place for a good year, except that I was increasingly incapacitated in my movement control while playing.

1985-AGED 31

In January I thought it was a good idea to try to become a PGA tutor, giving swing instruction to young assistants at training courses. I assisted tutors in sessions at Lilleshall and Sheffield, and came to the conclusion that it wasn't for me. It was interesting working with leading coaches such as John Sterling, but I found the PGA syllabus too restricting, not allowing for any personal input. Some of the swing ideas I didn't agree with, which made promoting them to the students impossible. It may be different now, but I was not impressed then.

By mid-March I was preparing for another foreign Pro-am trip, this time to Spain for the Midland PGA's event. We were to play one round at El Paraiso and two at Sotogrande New, which in future would be transformed into Ryder cup venue, Valderrama. The opening round was at El Paraiso, and on a cool and windy day in Spain my new playing season began. For 12 holes I swung beautifully, going out in an amazing 31 and starting back par, par, birdie, but for the last six holes I couldn't swing at all! Throughout the round my putter was red-hot, and using only 24 putts I made seven birdies to shoot a six under par 65. This was a course record and gave me a four stroke lead on the field. What a start to 1985!

Unfortunately, the shaky swinging continued and the great putting didn't, and on a tough course like Sotogrande in windy conditions the score would inevitably mount up. I struggled to two rounds of 79, but my total of 223 was still good enough for second place, four shots behind Angus Dow, and a useful £520 cheque. It was a rollercoaster ride of a tournament, but the 65 was encouraging.

Over the winter one of my assistants, Ben Adams, had decided he wanted to concentrate on playing and reduce his shop hours. Fortunately, I was able to call on retired member, Tom Baker to help out, and together with assistant Lee Bashford, they would keep the business running while I was away playing.

In late March I was again having a crack at the Sunningdale Foursomes, this time with Ben Adams. We managed to win our first match, but went out in the second round. Playing Sunningdale was always a pleasure and I am sure it was a great experience for Ben. There was nothing much to play in during April and it was on May 6th that my season resumed at the superb setting of St. Pierre in South Wales for the Welsh Rugby Union Pro-am. Feeling a little uneasy about my dystonia, I was expecting this to be a low-key affair where I could play round quietly without being noticed. When I arrived I couldn't believe all the razzamatazz; there were people everywhere, marquees, tv cameras, press-men. It was just like a major tournament. The reason for all the excitement was not only the presence of some top Pros, but also the celebrities who would be in the teams. My famous partners were comedian Lance Percival and rugby star Jeff Squire. With Lance's jokes coming thick and fast the round took an excruciating five and a half hours and with my form coming and going, I shot 75, including five birdies, to finish down the field.

Struggling with my swing in my next four events, it was at the Shifnal Pro-am where things came good again. On slow and bumpy greens a one under par 70 containing four birdies put me second, winning £175. Two days later, at a cool and drizzly Copt Heath, I kept it going with a steady level par 71 to again finish runner-up and pick up a welcome £300.

Before the end of May there would be a rare appearance in a tour event. The European Tour had decided to invite the top three players from each region of the PGA to the PGA Championship, and as I had finished third in the Midlands in '84, I was in the field at Wentworth. With brother Andrew on the bag, it was great to bring the old partnership together again, and we were determined to enjoy the experience. I shared a practice round with Midlands colleague Jim Rhodes and Australians Wayne (Radar) Riley and Greg Turner. Wayne was a great character who hit the ball miles and called a spade a spade. An interesting incident happened during practice, when I gave Seve Ballesteros a putting lesson! I was on the putting green chatting to South African John Bland, when Seve, who was practising nearby, asked us to look at his putting stroke, as it wasn't working too well. Rather taken aback that one of the game's icons would choose to ask my advice about his great putting action, I suggested that he was aiming a bit left. Better not tell him anything too extreme, I thought!

Paired with Teinie Britz and John Hoskisson, I made a very shaky start, only hitting one green on the front nine and going out in 40. With the course playing long and the greens very fast, it wasn't easy, but all of a sudden I began swinging well and hit every green coming back with a one under par 36 for a 76. While playing the 14th, 15th and 16th, the BBC cameras covered our group extensively and luckily I made three regulation pars drawing approval from Tony Jacklin, while Bruce Critchley was not so sure, saying that I 'did not have the best swing in the world'. They say any publicity is good publicity! I was lying in 54th place, just OK for the cut if I could maintain it, but anything could happen with my game these days. Round two started on a warmer day and I began in spectacular fashion with a holed bunker shot on the long par-four first for a birdie. I then had a nightmare on the quick greens with no less than six three-putt greens on the front nine. This gave me a disastrous 41 and a great back nine would be required. Although I improved and did make two more birdies, 38 was the best I could do for a 79. My 155 total missed the cut by four shots. With just average putting on the first nine I would have easily got through.

My nice sponsored car had now been returned, unfortunately, due to 'economic conditions', but it was great for the six months that it lasted. I now had a new deal with Sutton Park Renault for a subsidised rental on a sponsored car that still saved me some money.

The week after the PGA we hosted the Warwickshire Pro's Championship at Sutton Coldfield. Two days before I again visited Martin Hall for a lesson. My dystonia was causing strange things to happen in my swing; the weakness in my left arm and hand was making the right side dominant and my plane was all over the place. My swing had more planes than British Airways! In previous years I am confident I would have walked away with the title on my home course, but now I wasn't so sure of myself, and it showed in my first round finish. A creditable one under par with four holes to play, I then went bogey, bogey, par, double-bogey for a 75 to be in 10th place, six shots off the lead. Determined to get back into contention, I hit the ball well in the afternoon round, but 35 putts restricted my score to 72. My three over par total of 147 would be fourth, four shots behind the winner, collecting just £80.

I had an awful time in the Sandwell Pro-am. Level par after nine, I had two sevens and a six coming back and finished in 79. A similar experience was to follow in the Walmley Pro-am and my confidence became non-existent. Just when I was thinking it was all over and I should hang up my spikes, I played three excellent rounds at Staverton Park. The conditions were cool, windy and wet for the

Pro-am and subsequent Midland Pro's championship, decidedly unfavourable to me! In the Pro-am I had a great ball-striking day, hitting 11 of 14 fairways and 17 of 18 greens. The putting total of 34 was disappointing but my two under par 69 finished in top spot to take £150 first prize. In the tournament proper I didn't play quite so impressively, but my rounds of 71 and 72 were good enough for third place, only one behind winner Kevin Hayward who beat Andy Griffiths in a play-off. A cheque for £400 was my reward.

In late June we had a lovely family week away in Tenby, at our usual hotel by the beach. It was great to spend a week together without my having to go home halfway through for a tournament. On returning it was the Telford Ironmasters, one of my favourite events. This year the course was playing long and it was windy and cool. In the opening round I played fairly well for a 74 to be in seventh position, but it included an unfortunate one stroke penalty on the second when my ball moved after addressing it on the green. On day two, despite being shaky, I improved to a 70, but everybody seemed to play well and my level par total of 144 finished only 10th. In the Pro-am, although I started par, eagle and finished with a birdie, I could only score 73, which didn't finish well.

Mid-July and it was again time to mix with the stars, firstly in the Lawrence Batley at the Belfry and then at the Open qualifying at Princes, both venues where I had done well before. I was in the field at the Belfry due to an invitation for my top-three finish in the '84 Midlands order of merit; the tour had now dispensed with its pre-qualifying rounds. In the Batley I couldn't swing or putt due to the dystonia and shouldn't have really played in that condition. My embarrassing rounds of 81, 82 were nowhere near the cut. I was a little better in the Open qualifying at Princes, but never really showed the necessary control. In very windy conditions I missed out by only three shots with 77, 76.

Back in the lower division I started to regain some form. In a Pro-am at Ladbrook Park a one under par 70 put me in second place, one behind the winner. Two days later, at one of my favourite courses (not really!), Mickleover, I couldn't quite match last year's 63, but a three under par 66 was again good enough to win first prize. I had made six birdies and needed only 29 putts. In these two events I had won £360.

Next day I was in Shropshire at Hill Valley for the annual 36-hole Pro-am, which had been a good event for me before and would be again this year. With Rosie caddying I had a steady first round, except for a six on the first and a seven on the fifth. My two over par 74 was a long way off the pace, but my team was strongly in contention with a score of 130. On day two I made a great start with birdies on the first and fourth to be out in one under par 36, and began the back nine with another birdie. After a bogey on 13, a tremendous eagle three on the 16th helped me to a three under par 69. My 36-hole total of 143 put me in fourth spot, three behind winner Mike Slater. We had another fine team effort in the second round for a 128, which was good enough to be first-placed team in the Pro-am. A pleasing £570 was my reward and my hot spell continued.

On Sunday of the same week was the Worcestershire Pro-am at Malvern, and with the course in excellent condition, I found swinging hard work, but compensated with some great short game play to shoot a level par 71 to come in joint runner-up. Picking up another £170, I was now eagerly anticipating the Bena Cup, a new 36-hole Midland PGA tournament at Patshull Park the following week. Getting underway at the picturesque venue, it soon became apparent that the greens were not up to standard, but it didn't seem to affect me at all. My opening was nothing short of spectacular with a birdie four on the first and an eagle three on the second with a chip-in from 20 yards. Par on the third was followed with another birdie on the par-four fourth. This standard couldn't last since my swing was quite shaky and unpredictable, but I held it together well enough to score a two under par 70 to put me in third place, five off the lead held by Kevin Dickens. Round two started in a similar way to the first round, with two-putt birdies on the first and second and a long putt birdie three on the third. After three pars I then made more birdies on the seventh and eighth and with a par on the ninth reached the turn in a five under par 32. News was filtering across the course that Kevin Dickens was struggling and I knew I must be somewhere near the lead. A bogey on the 10th was more than made up for by birdies on 11 and 12. A few struggling holes followed, but a great 1 iron close to the flag on the long par-three 18th gave me an easy par. It was a 68 and my six under par 138 total gave me a two stroke victory in the tournament. A nice £500 cheque and a cut glass trophy were mine!

Now on a real high, I was looking forward to the Wilson Club Pro's Championship at The Belfry in early August. Being a Wilson staff player I was invited to a pre-tournament Pro-am. Off forward tees I played very well for a three under par 70 to be second, just one behind PGA champion Paul Way. That evening I had dinner in the company of world-wide Wilson boss, American George Napier and top retailing Pro John Reay from Coventry, which made for some fascinating conversation. The Belfry was in superb condition in preparation for the Ryder Cup, which would be held there in three weeks time and I was hopeful my recent form would stay with me.

Blustery conditions would prevail all week, which made the course even tougher than usual and from the farthest back tees it became clear that scoring would not be low. Starting on the 10th for round one I began bogey, birdie. The day continued in the same vein and despite making five birdies, I would finish in a three over par 76, just making the top twenty. On the second day, despite struggling with my swing, I drove well and made a fine start. With birdie threes on the second and sixth, I got to two under par, but three putts on the par-three seventh brought a bogey and with a further dropped shot on the eighth, I would go out in level par 37. A birdie three from close range on the 11th again took me under par, but a bogey on the short 14th returned me to even par. Still level standing on the 18th tee, I proceeded to finish with a double-bogey six for the second consecutive day. Very disappointing, but the Belfry's 18th hole must be one of Britain's hardest finishing holes, with carries over water for the first and second shots, followed by a fiendishly difficult green.

Now lying 11th, going into the third round I was fairly confident of keeping the momentum going, and on a dry, windy day this would be the case. I would hit the ball great most of the way round and although my putting stroke would hold up well on the quick greens, single putts would be rare commodities today. Tee to green on the front nine I could hardly have been better, hitting every fairway and only missing one green in regulation, but taking 18 putts meant that 38 was the best I could do. After nine holes like that on such a tough course, expectations are high that some birdies might follow on the back nine, but the round would continue in the same way, with just a solitary birdie on the par-four 13th and a couple of bogeys. Arriving at the 18th two over par today, I was hoping to improve on the double-bogeys of the previous rounds, and was relieved to make a regulation par this time. My 75 gave me a 54-hole score of 226 to be in 10th place, seven shots behind Robin Mann, but I knew that on a course like this things could change very quickly.

The final round would take place on Saturday August 10th on a windy and showery day. I was drawn to play in one of the later groups with Midland colleagues John Gould and Phil Hinton, and had attracted a small gallery of local supporters from Sutton Coldfield. If I was to mount a challenge, I needed one of my fast starts, but it didn't quite happen that way. A steady par four on the first was followed by a disappointing bogey on the short par-four second. I made amends for that with a long putt birdie after a fine long iron approach to the lengthy par-four third. Two pars followed and then a hugely disappointing three-putt bogey five on the sixth was a setback. Good birdie chances were narrowly missed on the seventh and eighth and it was beginning to look like it was not my day. Chatting to Phil Hinton as we walked along, he said that he thought I was turning my shoulders a little faster than usual through the downswing; in other words coming off the shot. Taking this on board, I hit a nice drive down the par-four ninth and then flushed a 6 iron straight at the flag which was in its toughest position on the right side of the green, just over the water. My ball pitched and stopped inches from the hole for a tap-in birdie to put me out in level par 37.

As we passed the score-board on our way to the 10th tee, it was apparent that nobody, apart from Robin, was scoring low and a good back nine could be very handy. After a nice par on the tricky 10th, I launched a drive down the 11th fairway, leaving a wedge shot to the green. Making another perfect contact with the ball, my approach again homed in on the flag and left me the shortest of putts for another birdie. Now one under for the round, the momentum was temporarily lost with a dropped shot on the long par-three 12th, but was soon re-discovered with a successful long birdie putt on the next hole. With a par on the 14th I found myself one below par with four holes to play. Missing the fairway on the par-five 15th, a recovery from the rough left me with a wedge to the green. A fine pitch to 12 feet was followed with a successful birdie putt. An excellent iron shot approach to the par-four 16th left me another good chance, but this time I was unable to convert and it was on to the par-five 17th. Being a sharp dog-leg to the right, the tee shot here is all-important, and I did well to put my drive on the fairway. A fine 3 wood second left me just in front of the green and a neat chip and putt produced another birdie. The final tee shot at the Belfry is nerve-wracking enough in a friendly four-ball, but in this situation it becomes formidable. However, managing to keep the gremlins at bay, I hit a reasonable drive that finished on the fairway, but too far right to be ideal. I was now left with a very difficult choice. It was a long carry over the water to get to the green, right on the limit for my 3 wood, but a lay-up seemed a negative choice. I knew I was close to the lead and may never get another chance as good as this to win a big tournament. I went with the 3 wood and with much will-power just managed to carry the lake. The ball duly followed instructions and ran up the green, halting pin-high on the middle level, 30 feet from the hole. Two putts later I was round in a three under par 70. I had played the back nine in 33 and had completed the last 10 holes in an amazing four under par!

All I could do now was watch the others finish, and everyone seemed to be struggling. The one exception was Robin Mann, who completed a superb performance with a birdie on the last for a 72 and a total of 291. My 296 put me in joint second place with Peter Allan, and my final round of 70 was the day's best score by two shots. I was very grateful to Phil Hinton for his timely advice; he had shot 78 to come in 16th. Rosie brought Emily and Christopher to see the presentation and when I went forward to accept my envelope, five-year old Emily said out loud that Daddy had been given a birthday card! Rather than containing a birthday card, inside the envelope was a cheque for £1,425, my biggest ever in a single event. Little Christopher didn't really know what was going on, but I think he knew Dad had done something good with all those people clapping and smiling at him! We celebrated by having a family meal out at a local restaurant, and I couldn't wait to get out and play again.

Rather unfortunately, the PGA's of Britain and the USA had recently decided to make the annual PGA Cup a biennial event and there would not be a match in 1985. The team for '86 would be made up of the nine players with the best combined finishes over the two intervening championships. I still had a good chance of making that team, but it would have been nice to make my second PGA Cup appearance in 1985.

Just four days later I was at Branston for a 36-hole Midland tournament. Feeling confident, I was dismayed to be subjected to awful weather conditions, heavy showers and very strong winds, conditions which never suited me. Taking account of the weather I did well to shoot two rounds of two over par 75 to finish in 15th place. A few days later we had a Pro-am at Kings Norton and with the inclement August weather continuing the course was muddy and playing long. Making one of my characteristically fast starts, I got to three under par after just four holes. Things deteriorated after that, but with a double-birdie finish, my level par 72 was good enough for joint first place, winning £165.

This was a busy week containing five Pro-ams and the next one was at nearby Tamworth Drayton Park, a course I hadn't played before. On a very windy afternoon I would hit the ball superbly all the way round. The stats speak for themselves; 13 of 15 drives on fairway, 15 of 18 greens hit in regulation including one par-five hit in two shots. The putting total of 33 was disappointing, but the greens were poor on the day. My one under par 70 finished joint first and won £150. Two days later was our own Second-City Pro-am at Sutton, which was now purely a team event with no individual competition. I played well over the 36 holes, making seven birdies, again picking up a useful cheque. A few hours later I was off to Llangollen on a very wet Friday to take the last tee-time of 3.20 in their Pro-am. It characteristically poured with rain the whole way round making the course play long and we had to play the last two holes in the dark, but remarkably enough I continued to play well, hitting 17 greens in regulation for a one under par 70. This put me in fifth place netting another three-figure prize. My form then dipped over the next fortnight. The cold, wet and windy weather was making the courses play long and most greens were poor.

Mid-September brought some improvement in the weather and my game. In the Midland President's Trophy at Kidderminster I made five birdies, including three twos for a 71 to come in fifth for £160. I really struggled in the Warwickshire Pro's Championship at the Forest of Arden, scoring 78, 76 to be seventh, a poor performance when I was probably favourite to win. Then at the Radcliffe-on-trent Pro-am I finished fifth with a 71 to pick up over £100. I was very pleased to see my assistant Ben Adams shoot a fine 67 to win this one.

In the Saab 54-hole Midland event at Cold Ashby I played fairly well to score 69, 73, 69 on the par 70 course in cool, breezy conditions to finish in seventh place and pick up over £100. In the first round at Cold Ashby David Dunk shot an incredible 61 that made my 69 feel quite poor!

I was finding it increasingly hard to swing smoothly and my round at Stratford on September 29th was typical of the period. Starting on the 10th in their Pro-am, I began superbly, hitting it close on the first three holes and birdieing two of them. Things continued well and a two-putt birdie four on the 18th put me out in 34, three under par. As I began my back nine on the first I started to get very shaky indeed and could barely swing at all. On the entire nine holes I hit only one fairway and two greens, but with some amazing recovery play I came back in level par 35, with just 11 putts! I finished second Pro and brought in the winning team to pick up nearly £200, but the celebrations were somewhat tainted for me by that worrying spell of dystonia.

Three days later we had a 72-hole Midland tournament, the Chorlton Cup at Belmont in Hereford. Throughout the event the wind blew and combined with some severe showers made for very trying conditions. Without being on top form, I gave a reasonable account of myself to score 76, 77, 75, 76 to end up in sixth place. My reward was £200 plus a bonus of £300 for finishing second in the Midland PGA order of merit for 1985, behind champion David Dunk. The winner of the Belmont tournament was Joe Higgins by an impressive margin of nine shots. Joe was a talented player always based around the Wolverhampton area, six years younger than me and our paths would cross many times over the years. He was renowned for his low-flying sand-wedge shot that would have a couple of bounces and invariably come to an abrupt halt by the flag. Always unlucky with injuries, but when fit Joe was a match for anybody.

Two horrific rounds would follow at Hill Valley and Hinckley where I just couldn't swing at all, but there was yet to be another highlight in this year's golf. The Warwickshire PGA Match-Play Championship, which I had won in 1980, was this year at Leamington. For mid-October the weather was remarkably kind to us, but the course was wet and playing long. I comfortably qualified with a two over par 73 and was drawn against Alan Partridge from Moor Hall in the opening round. The first hole went my way with a birdie four, but the match was tight and we turned all square. I then played some solid golf and finally prevailed three and two. Round two produced a classic match against Andy Bownes. Andy's huge hitting could be quite intimidating, but if I could just play my own game I fancied my chances against him. I lost the first to a birdie and the sixth to a par to be two down. I won the seventh and the ninth with pars and Andy won the eighth with a birdie. Andy's power was a big advantage in the heavy conditions and when he won the 13th to go two up, things were looking bad. But suddenly I found another gear and after halving the 14th with a birdie four, I went on to win the last four holes, three of them with birdies to turn the match round and win by two holes. Andy must have been in shock!

The semi-final against Scott Gilmour only lasted 12 holes, the result being seven and six in my favour, allowing me some welcome rest before the afternoon's final against John Gould. This would be a similar affair to my first round contest with Alan Partridge. I won the first with a birdie and with some scrappy play, turned one up. I then played much better on the back nine, being one under par for the remaining holes to come out on top by three and two. I was delighted to get my name on the trophy for a second time and took the £190 first prize.

This had been a difficult year to assess; I had won over £7,000, more than in '84, in less rounds, 68 in all, but my stroke average of 73.7 was more than a full stroke per round worse. My performance in tour events and the Open had been abysmal, but I had finished runner-up in the Club Pro's Championship, winning my biggest ever prize. I had finished second in the Midland order of merit and was Warwickshire match-play champion for a second time, but didn't know from one day to the next if I would be able to swing smoothly or would be crippled by tremor. Generally speaking, I was better in small events than bigger ones, so my plan for '86 would be based on that. All thoughts of being a world-beating tour star had long gone. It was now a case of just doing the best I could.

On the home front, Emily was now six and Christopher three, so we decided they were old enough for a winter holiday and booked a week in Tenerife for mid-January. Things were ticking over at the club, but it was clear I would need a second full-time assistant, so a replacement was sought. There was never a shortage of applicants when I had a vacancy at Sutton and soon Mike Whitehouse was the new boy, who would start in March. Mike, a smart lad with a powerful swing always had a penchant for cars and eventually this would lure him away from golf.

1986–AGED 32

The year began with a long period of cold weather with very little golf. In fact, it would be March before I would start playing again. Our break in the Canaries was enjoyable, but didn't go entirely smoothly. We all suffered with tummy bugs at various times in the week and the hotel swimming pool, although visually enticing, was icy cold! My lasting memory of the holiday is of the kids having fun on the beach in the strangely black, volcanic sand.

One of the few Alliances I played that spring was the 36-hole foursomes at Coventry Finham. My partner from Sutton was keen competitor Derek Jones who played his part admirably. Combining well throughout the day, we came out on top for an enjoyable victory.

With Mike now in place as assistant, I allowed him to take a very special pre-arranged holiday in April to Augusta, Georgia for The Masters. A relative had arranged tickets for Mike and his Dad and I was very jealous. This was Jack Nicklaus's famous final major victory aged 46 and Mike kindly brought me a Masters towel and draw-sheet which I have kept safely ever since.

My first event of any consequence was the Welsh Rugby Union Pro-am at St. Pierre in early May. Having played last year, I knew what to expect. I really shouldn't have played, as I was having a bad time with dystonia right through the game, and our match had a huge gallery because my celebrity partner was none other than Welsh comedian Max Boyce. Max was great fun, with a non-stop barrage of gags, but I was embarrassed with my play, finishing with a 77.

My next two Pro-ams were very much the same. At the Forest of Arden, after starting with two pars I had an awful spell where I could barely hit the ball at all, then made four birdies including two twos to finish on 77. Then at Shifnal I had the most horrific opening, with five straight bogeys to go out in 43, only to follow up with a steady back nine of 36. I sensed people were asking each other " What on earth has happened to Thorpy?" and I found it very difficult to explain that I had this unusual movement disorder that made it difficult to play. I just hoped I could play through it and mostly I could, but usually the damage had been done and the round would be beyond redemption.

Mid-May arrived and I had barely won a penny, but things would get temporarily better in the next two Pro-ams. On a cold and windy Sunday at Stourbridge, the course was nice, but I was finding it hard to swing. Fighting to hold my score together with some good short game play, I suddenly hit one close on the par-three seventh and made a two. Six on the ninth and five on the 11th didn't help but then a holed bunker shot for another two on the 12th improved the situation. From then on I got better and six straight par fours to finish gave me a 72 to put me in fifth place to win a welcome cheque for £120. The following day I was at Maxstoke Park and I was back to my old self. Hitting the ball well and swinging with control, I began with a birdie and got to four under par after 12 holes. I eventually completed the course in a three under par score of 68 to win by one shot. This was a new professional course record, but only won me £90 on the day.

A couple of days later I was off to Wentworth for another PGA Championship. Like last year I had been invited to play because of my top 3 finish in the Midland PGA order of merit. In my current state I should never have played, but an invitation like that was hard to refuse. Ian Barker, a university friend of my brother, kindly caddied for me, and I felt so sorry for him. From start to finish I had a dreadful time. I couldn't swing or putt without shaking and was in trouble the whole way round. Looking back on it now it all seems like a bad dream and I just wanted to get off the course as soon as possible. I could not have had this melt-down in a worse setting, with thousands of spectators and TV cameras watching. I did well to get round in two scores of 83, but of course finished comfortably in last place. This was to be my final appearance in a European Tour event and was undoubtedly the low point of my career to date, but worse was to come!

I never have been a quitter and a week later I was back on the first tee trying to find some kind of a game in a Pro-am at Rothley Park. My long game was dreadful and a reasonable score of 76 was achieved only with some remarkable scrambling. Early the next morning, Monday June 2nd, I was at Harborne Golf Club for the 36-hole Warwickshire Professional Championship, an event I had come very close to winning in previous years. This would be my final attempt and with confidence very low I didn't expect to succeed. It was a pleasantly warm day, but the course was in poor condition. Beginning tentatively, I managed to hold it together for a three over par round of 73 to be in fifth place at the lunch interval. Swinging much better in the afternoon, I hit the first 13 greens in regulation, reaching one under par. My last five holes were a bit scrappy, but with some deft recovery play, I managed to hold my score to finish with a fine 69. My 142 total put me in third spot, five shots behind champion Pip Elson. The £112 I won was a welcome addition to the meagre rewards so far this year. The following afternoon saw me at Notts Golf Club, Hollinwell for a Pro-am. On a windy day, with the greens unusually bumpy for this great course, I never got going and scored a poor 79.

Three more Pro-ams the following week brought mixed results. At Sandwell Park, that fine test of heathland golf set improbably next to the M5, I played well, only missing three greens in regulation to get round in level par 71. This put me in third place and with my team coming in second, I picked up over £100. A poor 78 at Ladbrook Park brought little reward and at Walmley I couldn't swing properly, resulting in a fruitless round of 75.

In late June we took a family break in Tenby. It was great to get away and enjoy the seaside with Rosie and the kids. It was becoming clear that tournament winnings were going to be increasingly difficult to come by and with a growing family to consider, some thought had to be given to the future.

Immediately on returning, I faced four consecutive days of play. The weather had turned hot and my game had also improved. In a small Pro-am at Moor Hall I made five birdies to shoot a level par 70 and bring in the winning team. I then moved on to Mickleover, one of my most successful, if not favourite venues. As a team, I don't think we featured, but I played some good stuff after a slow start, making six birdies in the last 13 holes for a two under par 67 to come in fourth and take a prize of £130. To date, I have only played Mickleover three times, in 1984, '85 and '86 and scored 63, 66 and 67 for a total of 11 under par!

The high temperatures continued as I moved to Enville for a 36-hole Midland tournament. Enville has two fine courses which wind their way through silver birch and heather. Just my kind of course, but strangely I have never done well there. This was to be one of my better Enville performances, steady rather than spectacular. Over the two rounds I avoided taking more than five on any hole and also never took more than two putts on any green to score 74, 72 and finish 11th.

Another of my best courses was Telford, but for this year's Ironmasters I was too tremulous to do well. It began promisingly with a birdie three on the first, but it didn't last and I would eventually score 73, 76 to finish down the field. The Pro-am, however, was a different story. It was a complicated round and deserves some analysis. Making a great start with birdies on the second, fourth, fifth and ninth to go out in four under par 32, thoughts of my 1983 course record 62 in this same event inevitably came flooding back. Three steady pars to start back were followed by two disastrous sixes on the par-five 13th and par-four 14th. Quickly getting over that setback, I made a birdie three on the 15th and a birdie four on the 17th to get to three under par on the final tee. Not able to hit the 18th fairway, I would take a bogey five to shoot a two under par 70. A very eventful round containing six birdies put me in third place and with my team coming in second I picked up over £100. This round was typical of my better performances at that time, very inconsistent with birdies and bogeys equally liable to occur. I was definitely not a boring golfer!

Once the Telford presentation was over, I was on the road northwards with the forlorn hope of playing in another Open Championship. It was to be at Turnberry this year and my allotted qualifying course was Barrassie, a fine links sharing the same stretch of land as Western Gailes and Glasgow Gailes, courses I knew from past Opens. Getting on to the Open's starting grid was becoming progressively harder as its popularity grew. When I first qualified in 1976 there were 719 entries and in this year of 1986 there was a total of 1,347 excellent players trying to be among the 150 or so elite who would tee off in The Open proper. There were 15 places available on my course as I set off in perfect conditions on Sunday afternoon. After a bogey, birdie start, I played steadily to be out in 36, not far off the pace. A double-bogey six on the 10th knocked me back and with a bogey five on the 14th and a birdie three on the 18th I would finish the first round with a three over par 74. To have any chance of qualifying I would need a sub-par second round, and this was well within my capabilities. Monday's round got underway very much like the previous one with a bogey five on the first and a birdie four on the third to be level par after four holes. Then disaster; I contrived to make two consecutive sixes on par-fours to put myself completely out of contention! Although I subsequently completed the remaining holes in even par, the damage was done. My score of 149 was eight shots off the qualifying score and it felt that, sadly I would never play in a fifth Open.

There was no time to feel sorry for myself, and after watching Greg Norman on TV take the claret jug in his usual spectacular style, I was soon on my way to Southport for the Wilson Club Pro's Championship at the superb Royal Birkdale. Hopefully, the great links course that I knew so well from previous adventures would prove inspirational. My start in Wednesday's first round was anything but confidence building and I would be four over par after only three holes. However, I knew how difficult Birkdale was and if I could just steady the ship a little, things would be OK. With scrappy play I found myself on the 17th tee seven over par, but then somehow found some good swings to birdie both remaining par-fives for a 77. Starting round two on the cut mark, I was determined to be better today and made a great start by birdieing my opening hole, the par-four 10th. Some really solid striking would follow and I reached the turn in level par 37, only to spoil things with a double-bogey six on the first. Again picking up the baton, I played well all the way in to make seven pars and a fine birdie two on the seventh, to shoot a one over par 73. On a cool and breezy Friday morning I set off for my third round in 28th position. The fast greens were very tricky in the strong wind and although I still hit a number of good shots, my 37 putts meant I could do no better than 78. The final round would be an anti-climax after last year's excitement at the Belfry, but I still intended to try my hardest to put a score together on one of my favourite courses. A bogey, bogey start didn't help and further bogeys on the seventh and ninth put me out in 39. Coming home for the final time I put together my best nine holes of the event marred only by three putts on the 15th. Birdies on the final two holes would give me a 36, one under par for the back nine for a respectable 75. My 303 total put me in lowly 40th place to win just £130, but it had been fun to play Birkdale again. There would be no PGA Cup for me as my combined positions of second and 40th were too far down the list.

I was then presented with what should have been a great chance to win the 36-hole Midland Pro's Championship. That opportunity was simply that it was being held at Sutton Coldfield, my home course. Had it been two or three years earlier, I would have felt odds-on favourite to take the title on a course where I had played so many great rounds, but now I wasn't so sure. I was shaky, a much shorter hitter than previously and an unreliable putter. Apart from that, I was OK! In late July unseasonably cold, windy and wet weather cruelly set in, but my opening round began in fine style. Hitting eight of the first nine greens in regulation I reached the turn in even par 37. An irritating three-putt-bogey five on the easy 10th was followed by a great birdie three on the demanding 11th. Two scrambled pars led to another birdie on the par-five 14th. Missing the green on the par-three 15th, I again got up and down for par and found myself on the 16th tee one under par, which had to be close to the lead in the trying conditions. But the wheels were about to come well and truly off on this par-four dog-leg left hole. After visiting the trees off the tee, I would single putt for a six! Following a solid par on the short 17th, I hit two nice shots on to the 18th only to take three putts for a bogey five. It all added up to 74, and while only four shots off the lead, left me in 17th position in the bunched field. Looking forward to breaking away from the group in the final round, I was to be frustrated by the weather, as the torrential rain caused the second round to be cancelled and the championship was decided over 18 holes. Bad luck for me, but inconsistent play had let me down again.

The wet weather continued for a Pro-am at Glen Gorse in Leicester, where I was to suffer a humiliating day. Struggling to hold the club and unable to control my swing, I shot 82 to finish in last place. Two days later in a similar event at Kingsthorpe in Northampton, the sun came out and my swing returned. A level par 70 left me in fourth spot, winning £70, not much but at least it was an improved performance.

A very different five-day excursion, a Dutch adventure to the International Broekpolder Golf Tournament for Club Professionals in Rotterdam would follow. This was a select, invitational event and I was requested to be one of the 37 players. It was an 'expenses paid' trip with a small prize guaranteed and no cut in the 72 holes. Just my kind of tournament, I thought, in my current state! Four of us Brits; myself, David Dunk, Stuart Brown and Tim Giles flew out from Heathrow and the rest of the field, mainly from continental Europe, joined us at the club. The Dutch members were most hospitable and the course, although flat, was very testing with water coming into play on many occasions. Over the four rounds, I never really played well, scoring 79, 80, 77, 77 to be 25 over par on 313. Only one player, Stuart Brown, broke 300 and his 299 finished two shots ahead of the field. I came in 10th to win £320.

On returning home my performances in the next two Pro-ams were so poor that I would win no money in either. This was a new and unwelcome trend and one I wanted to reverse as soon as possible. In a big Pro-am at Kings Lynn I was a little better. Despite a seven to start and a six on the 18th I shot 76 on the difficult track to be 11th Pro, and with fourth-placed team, picked up £190. Early the following morning I was off on the long drive to Llangollen for their Pro-am. "Would it be raining again?" I wondered. Guess what, it was pouring! It always rained at Llangollen. Wet conditions were bad news for me these days, as my grip on the club was getting less and less secure. However, I coped well in the wet and scored a creditable 73, but finishing in 25th place brought little reward.

Becoming increasingly disillusioned with my game, a week without my clubs seemed to do some good, and in the Robin Hood Pro-am on the last day of August, I swung the club very well, hitting 16 greens in regulation. A one under par 71 gave me third place and a cheque for £110. Two days later we had the Warwickshire Open at the Belfry. With the course set up very challenging and a brisk wind, it was obvious that scoring would be high. I shot 83, 79, which sounds horrific, but even with those scores I would finish fifth Pro, 10 shots behind winner Peter McEvoy.

A disappointing Second-City Pro-am at Sutton would follow where I scored 74 to be 15th. In mid-September we were back at Cold Ashby for a 54-hole Midland event. In unusually balmy conditions for such an exposed location, I had a very topsy-turvy tournament, making 10 birdies, including four twos, and no less than five sixes. My scores were 76, 72, 69 on the par 70 course to finish 12th and win a small prize. Just after I was to receive another shock to the system in a Pro-am at Stratford. On a lovely warm day, at a course that I liked, my dystonia was so bad with my driver that I could only hit one out of 13 fairways off the tee. Incredibly, the rest of my game was quite good, and with the rough light, I was able to get round in even par 72 to finish fifth. Not knowing whether to laugh or cry, I was to suffer a similar experience in a Pro-am at Longcliffe soon after. Scoring a terrible 81 myself, my team came in with a great score of 130 to come out on top, winning me £200!

Winning so little money as I had this year, things were becoming tighter financially, and since I was no longer the local star player, my car sponsorship had gone. Forced to buy a car, I decided on a nearly new Austin Maestro, a choice that I am sure would bring hoots of derision from my son in the future. It was, however, voted car of the year at that time! I picked it up on Emily's seventh birthday. I am sure this wouldn't have interested her at all, as she would be too busy with her friends and presents, but her little brother would have been fascinated, since he was fast becoming a car expert, even at three years old!

At the end of September, I partnered Jim Rhodes in the Midland Four-ball Championship at the Forest of Arden. Jim, a little older than me, had been a successful Midlands and Staffordshire player for some time and in the future would become successful on the European Seniors Tour. We made a good team, and in the qualifying round scored a fine five under par 67 to jointly lead the field. Our first round opponents were Mike Welsh and Russell Price, who we managed to beat comfortably five and four. We then had a great match with the Hinton brothers, Paul and Phil and just prevailed by one hole. Having progressed to the semi-final, we then came up against tour players David Russell and Mark Mouland. My outstanding memory of this match is that we were consistently out-driven by both opponents by up to 70 yards as they powered to victory by four and three. Jim and I had played well throughout the four rounds, bogeying only one hole and finishing up 16 under par in all.

There would be two more match-play events before the close of the season, the Midland and Warwickshire championships. Over the years I had been quite successful in match-play, and if I could manage to swing and putt with some control, I thought I could mount challenges in both of these tournaments. The Midland match-play was to be held at Kings Norton in Birmingham, and in mid-October the course was likely to be long and wet, not my favourite conditions. Surprisingly, it would turn out to be mostly cool, crisp and sunny autumn weather, but my first match started badly. Starting on the

10th against Bob Larratt, I found myself three down after eight holes, but as we turned for home, I started to find some form. Winning the first, second, third and fourth , two of them with birdies, I was in front for the first time. Losing the fifth to a par, I then won the sixth and seventh with pars to be dormie 2 up. Bob won the eighth with a par, but after halving the last in par fives I came out on top by one hole.

Round two would be against David Russell, who had recently given me a beating at the Forest of Arden in the Midland four-ball. David was a star at Kings Norton, and with his pictures adorning the clubhouse he attracted quite a local gallery for our match. With my now funny, wobbly swing, I was no match for Dave's big hitting, but with my short irons and putting working well it was going to be close contest. Even par for the front nine, and with several holes having changed hands I was one up at the turn. After winning the 10th in par to go two up, losing the 11th to a par was a blow, but from then on I played some great stuff. 12 and 13 were halved in par and the 14th was shared in birdie twos. The 15th was halved with pars, then D. J. won the 16th with a birdie three. With the contest evenly balanced on the 17th tee, the match was about to reach a dramatic conclusion. David hit a solid iron shot on to the par-three green, while my 6 iron shot missed the green right and seemed to disappear into the ditch that guards the green. On reaching the scene, my ball was miraculously sitting on wooden sleepers which formed a bridge over the water hazard. Only about 20 yards from the flag, and with a clear route to the hole, I putted off the bridge right to the hole-side and came out with a lucky half. On the uphill par-five 18th, I then dramatically holed from 30 feet for a match-winning birdie to win one-up. I had been one under par for the match and would now face Mike Gallagher in the quarter-final.

Mike was always a gritty little competitor, with a surprisingly long backswing and very effective putting stroke. In another close match my long game started poorly, but improved towards the end. Mike's putter was on fire for 11 holes, making seven single putts, but then cooled considerably and he could hole nothing after that. I was one down at the turn and after halving 10 and 11 in pars, a birdie three on the 12th levelled the match. The 13th was shared in par and after a great short iron to the short 14th, a birdie from close range put me in front for the first time. Then, crucially, Mike's tee shot went missing in the trees on the 15th to enable me to go two up. The 16th and 17th were halved in pars to give me a two and one victory. This was turning into a good tournament for me and I was now only two wins away from the title.

My semi-final opponent was old Warwickshire rival Phil Weaver, who would be tough to beat. With a 7.50 tee-time it was still cold and frosty as we began. Phil took the first with a par four, but I won the next two holes in par. After four holes halved with pars, Phil won the eighth with a par and we turned on level terms. I had not swung at all well so far, but as in previous rounds, things improved on the back nine. We halved the tricky 10th in birdie threes and I took the 12th and 13th with fine birdies to go two up. Phil fought back with birdies of his own on the 14th and 16th and with both of us parring 17 and 18 the tie would have to be decided in sudden-death. After halving the first in pars, Phil's par four on the second would be good enough to prevail. It was a close match of high-class golf which could have gone either way, but I had been pleased with my performance and collected £400 for my third place finish. I had also finished third in the Midland PGA order of merit.

That order of merit position ended a run of six consecutive years in the top three, including two first places, of which I was very proud. Unknown to me at the time, that third place at Kings Norton in 1986 would be my last high finish of any kind in an individual event at higher than county level. Inability to control my movement was catching up with me fast, but I was still competitive and would keep trying until the end.

The final event of my year would be the Warwickshire match-play championship at Coventry Hearsall. As holder of the title and twice the champion, I wanted to make a good defence of the trophy, but knew it would be hard. The Birmingham Evening Mail said I was 'hot favourite', but it certainly didn't feel that way. The qualifying round took place on a cold October day with heavy showers, lovely! Coping with the foul conditions surprisingly well, I chipped in from 30 yards for a birdie on the 18th to score 73 and finish in joint first place. In similar weather, I was up against Brian Barton in the first round and with a solid performance, came out on top by three and two. My afternoon quarter-final against Mark Chamberlain went very much the same way. Never behind, I won two and one and would meet Mark Warner in the semi-final next morning. On another miserable wet day, I struggled with my swing, only hitting three greens on the front nine to turn two down. Three winning birdies coming home put me back to all square on the final tee, but a nasty three-putt on the 18th green lost me the match. There was still more golf to be played in the afternoon with the third-place play-off against my own assistant Lee Bashford. When Lee went five up after 11 holes, it looked like I would be taking an early bath, but somehow I played the last seven holes in 2 under par to pull all five holes back and take the match to extra time. It was to be a similar outcome to my recent sudden-death play-off against Phil Weaver with Lee coming out on top with a winning par on the 20th. I had made a spirited defence, all things considered, and won £100 for my effort.

This would turn out to be my final Warwickshire PGA championship event, as I would soon be moving on. My record in the county Pro's stroke-play, match-play and open is worth examination and is one that I am proud of. Eight appearances in the Warwickshire Pro's stroke-play produced four top-three finishes, including once just failing to take the trophy in a play-off. Six attempts at the match-play brought four top-three finishes, including twice as champion. In six efforts at the Warwickshire Open I was three times in the leading three pros, including once losing out for the title in a play-off. With the alliances to play in the winter, the county fixtures had been an important part of my schedule at Sutton.

My play in 1986 could be best described as gritty and determined. I was now really having a hard time with my dystonia. One of the worst aspects was trying to explain myself to people as to why I wasn't the player I once was and why I would have spells where I appeared incredibly nervous but in fact the tremor was beyond my control. Taking that into account, I had done well to have a stroke average of 74.6 and win over £3,000, but this was much worse than in previous years, and if, as seemed likely, this trend continued, I would not be playing much tournament golf in future.

One consolation of not playing so well was that my schedule had quietened down considerably and I was able to spend more time at home with Rosie and the kids. Christopher was four in November and had recently started nursery school. Emily was now seven and a keen ballet dancer. They were great fun, but had not yet been introduced to golf. This would come next year. Rosie had played a bit and was knowledgeable about the game, but having seen the frustration golf causes, she didn't seem inclined to take it up.

10

GET ME OUT OF HERE

1987-AGED 33

Over Christmas we had decided that I should try for a new job. Although I had been happy for the past eight years at Sutton, the business had always been not much more than a base from which to launch my assault on the tournament circuit. As a stand-alone enterprise, even with support from the members, it didn't really work and with the poor teaching facilities, improvement seemed unlikely. The superb heathland Sutton Coldfield course had been perfect for the development of my game and looking back, I probably played better at Sutton than anywhere else.

I had considered work in golf sales, but no vacancies in the area had come up, so a better club pro's job seemed the best option. In February I applied for two positions; Sandiway Golf Club in Cheshire and Gog Magog Golf Club in Cambridge. I was soon called for interviews and both went well. I was asked to visit Gog Magog again; this time with my wife and my clubs! Rosie was nervous, but was fine. I was apprehensive, not so much about the business side of things, but about being so shaky that I would be unable to swing and making a fool of myself. Out on the course in cold and windy conditions with three committee members, I was very weak and tremulous and played quite poorly, but they just thought I was nervous and seemed to be impressed with me. The facilities at the Gogs were superb, with 27 holes, very large and conveniently placed practice ground and a nice, if compact shop. We liked Cambridge very much and thought it likely that I would take the job if offered it.

Two days later I was off to Spain for a Pro-am with three people I had played with in the previous year. My recollection of this trip is very sketchy, but I know I shot 76, 80, 74 and won £60. What I do remember is a call to Rosie when she told me I had been offered the Gogs job! I sent my acceptance and couldn't wait to get back to make all the arrangements. I would take over from Eddie Birchenough, who was moving to Royal Lytham, on May 1st and the next month would be incredibly hectic.

Eventually, all the arrangements were made. My assistant Lee would stay at Sutton and hope to work for my successor, which he did. His fellow-assistant Mike would leave to take up a career in car sales. Greg Schofield, low-handicap son of the stewardess at Sutton, would join me as assistant at Gog Magog, together with Neil Suckling, who had been working for Eddie. On Thursday afternoon, April 30th, we set off in convoy for East Anglia, Greg driving a van full of shop stock and Rosie and I in our cars.

After a massive effort by everyone, the shop was up and running at my busy, classy, new environment. The one thing I didn't really need at this time, was a Pro-am at the club where my performance would be the centre of attention among the members. But that was exactly what was scheduled four days after my arrival! With Rosie on the bag, and having hardly played for a month I set off apprehensively. In an up and down round, made up of lots of poor shots, several particularly good 7 iron shots and a number of single putts, I made five birdies to shoot a level par 70. Amazingly, in a field that included Robin Mann, Howard Clark and Ian Mosey, I would finish joint first with Robin to win £400. The local press said "Golf Professional David Thorp celebrated his arrival in Cambridge with a debut victory last night. The 34-year-old Yorkshireman, who took over at the Gog Magog club last Friday, was over the moon after tying for first place in his club's pro-am." That just about summed it up, but with my movement control deteriorating further, this was a playing standard I would be unable to maintain.

A week later, as fate would have it, I was back at Sutton Coldfield for a regional qualifying round of the Club Pro's championship. A round of 77, which was poor for me at Sutton, failed to qualify and marked the end of a remarkable run in the Club Professional's Championship of Great Britain and Ireland, to give it the full title. From 1977 to 1986, I had completed four rounds in all ten events, finishing in the top 25 five times, with best places being second in 1985 and seventh in 1980. I was to play once more, in 1988 at Royal St. David's, and a very ill-fated affair that would be.

Later in May, with our house in Aldridge now sold, the family moved into a flat in Victoria Road, Cambridge, while we waited for our house purchase in Harston to proceed. The flat was kindly loaned to us by Frank Matthews, a member at the club. This incredibly kind gesture, considering the high property prices in the area, gave us the ideal chance to get to know the city. Emily was able to move to the local Harston school and Christopher would follow in September. Things were going well at the club and in June we took a welcome family break in Tenby, before moving house. On August 27th we moved our posessions out of storage and into 32 The Limes, in the pleasant village of Harston, about three miles from the golf club, and everything was looking good.

Playing in a few regional and county events and a number of Pro/Captain matches at the club, I was struggling to put scores together, but my performances were just within the bounds of respectability. A 72 in a Pro-am at East Herts won £115 and rounds of 78, 74 at Dunstable Downs won me £50 in the Cambs. and Beds. Open. A small win of £110 for a 73 in a Pro-am at Cambridgeshire Hotel was my only other success that year. Towards the end of the year, I became quite bad and had some horrific experiences on the course, when I wished the ground would swallow me up. Even though it had been five years since my dystonia had been diagnosed, I still wasn't prepared for this disaster that was happening to me, and really couldn't cope with it. I would avoid contact with club members just in case they asked me about my game, and would tuck myself in a secluded corner of the enormous practice ground, hitting balls with the forlorn hope of my swing returning to its former self.

1988–AGED 34

We were enjoying life in Cambridge; Emily and Christopher were installed at their new school and Rosie had started a part-time job there helping pupils with learning difficulty. The city, with its wealth of history and famous university, was always interesting to visit and we were surrounded by beautiful, if flat, countryside. My shop business was much better than at previous clubs and my teaching reputation was growing. I had excellent relationships with two of the biggest golf companies that were locally based, Titleist and Spalding. On the surface everything was great, but my inability to play was eating away at me, and I felt on the verge of cracking up.

I made some confidential enquiries with golf companies about sales jobs, but with no success. I was trying to avoid playing, but the demands of the job made this impossible, and at the end of March we hosted the 36-hole Alliance Championship, which I had entered. Hitting balls on the practice ground prior to the first round, my swing was so out of control that I knew I wouldn't be able to play and for the first time in my career I would claim injury and withdraw from the tournament. It was going to be very difficult to come back from that, but I would have to play in our Pro-am in May. It seemed a long time ago since I had won it last year. I did play, but was unable to complete a score and would have an embarrassing 'no return'.

My excellent assistant Greg sensed something was badly wrong and decided to leave to take up a post with Tommy Horton at Royal Jersey. Greg would go on from there to ever more impressive Pro's positions; Dubai, Gleneagles and currently Sandy Lane in Barbados. His place was taken by a pleasant young man with the unusual name of Dalvyn Germaney. Neil had also left by this time and was replaced by Philip Rains, another capable assistant. In May half-term I was delighted to get away for yet another family week in Tenby and enjoy some seaside fun. By now both Emily and Christopher had started

*With Christopher, Emily and Reg Cox at Gog Magog practice ground,
Cambridgeshire, 1988.*

to have a few lessons with me on the practice ground and it was great to see them enjoying their efforts.

Three days after returning from holiday in South Wales I was off to North Wales for the 1988 Club Pro's Championship at Royal St. Davids in Harlech. I must have been able to claim an exemption from qualifying for some reason, because I certainly would not have been able to get through any kind of pre-qualifying given the state my game was in. I would normally have relished the opportunity to play on such a great links as Harlech, but it would turn out to be a disturbing experience. Right from the start I was unable to swing or putt with any control, and just managed to complete the first round in 85 to be dead last in the field. Considering my record in this event, that score must have been incomprehensible to most of my peers, but worse was to come. In round two I just couldn't take any more punishment after a while and retired hurt part way through the round. Leaving the course in a hurry, I returned to Barmouth, where I was staying, and went for a walk in the hills at the back of the town, which overlook the sea. It was a beautiful sunny evening and this was a place where Rosie and I had walked many times in the past. As I walked along the high rocks my whole career flashed through my mind as vague thoughts of how it would feel to jump off the edge entered my head. Fortunately, they didn't last long and soon I was back in the town finding some dinner and looking forward to returning home tomorrow. A turning point had been reached, and I couldn't see any way of playing golf again, never mind playing professionally.

After sadly walking off the course at Harlech in June 1988, I would not play competitively again until September 1989, a gap of 15 months. My professional playing career was effectively over, in fact it had realistically ended in autumn 1986 at the young age of 33. Between May 1970, when as a 17 year old I had played in the Graham Textiles tournament at Sandmoor and October 1986 at Hearsall when I was losing semi-finalist in the Warwickshire match-play, I had crammed in about 1,000 competitive rounds. Of those, 93 scores had been in the sixties, and 20 had been course records (some all-comers and some professional records), the best of which was probably the 10 under par 62 at Telford in 1983. My best annual scoring average had been 72.5 for 67 rounds in 1984. The surprising statistic, writing this in 2008, is that despite all that good play, my career winnings were under £50,000.

Prize-money in the big events has simply rocketed since I played in my last Open in 1983. My best Open placing was 49th pro in 1981 at Sandwich, for which I received £550. The same placed competitor in the 2006 Open at Hoylake was paid £12,250, a massive increase of 2,127%! The European Tour events and PGA Club Professional's Championship also pay out vastly more prize-money, but the regional tournaments and Pro-ams don't seem to have grown in the same proportions.

Although I probably could have stayed on at the Gogs, running the shop and giving lessons, I felt that playing golf was an integral part of the club pro's job. By now my alarming inability to swing the club was becoming seriously depressing, so I sadly decided to hand in my notice and develop a career in golf sales as an agent in the Midlands. We had a tremendous closing down sale, where I managed to sell nearly all the remaining stock. The members at Gog Magog were wonderfully kind and understanding and there are many happy memories from my time there.

The situation caused unfortunate domestic upheaval, but Rosie and the kids were incredibly supportive throughout. We put the house on sale and planned to move back to Bridgnorth, Rosie's home-town and the place where we had lived when first married. Emily and Christopher would have to leave their school in Harston, and Rosie would also lose her job at the school.

11

Encore?

1989-AGED 35

That winter was very tough, trying to sell goods for small, obscure golf companies was hard work. Living in Cambridge and covering the Midlands and North Wales meant driving ridiculous distances, but the Pros were quite supportive and bought from me when they could.

On February 8th, Derek Lawrenson, then golf correspondent for the Birmingham Post and now with the Daily Mail, met up with me at the Belfry to inform his readers of my recent fate. Derek has always been an entertaining and informative journalist and had written many pieces describing my successes in the past. He was surprised to hear my story and wrote in the Birmingham Post "David Thorp's clear blue eyes still shine with the memory of the days when he was one of the country's leading club professionals. He represented Great Britain and Ireland in the 1980 PGA Cup and led the Midland order of merit in each of the next two years. He had still to reach 30 and, in the normal run of things, would now, at 35, be at the height of his powers. Yet last week, as he hit golf balls on the driving range at the Belfry, there was nothing to distinguish Thorp's shots from those of the highest of handicap players. For years, Thorp has fought against a neurological condition known as dystonia. Watching his pitiful efforts, trying to reach out for what until recently was a swing that had earned him a useful living, it was clear that dystonia had won." It was hard to read that in the paper, but it really brought home what had happened to me.

Selling Harway clubs was hard and I needed a big name to sell, and fortunately one came along in the form of Ram, a well-respected, family-owned American golf company. With the Zebra putter and Tour Grind irons, Ram made quality equipment with which I was proud to be associated. Things got much better and with the help of sales manager Mike Osborne and managing director Stuart Barber, my income improved. By summer I still had not played any golf, and was due to go to the Open at Troon to work for Ram in the exhibition tent. It would be hard to be at the Open without my clubs, but it turned out to be an enjoyable experience, meeting up again with Tom Watson, Ram's top player, and watching him come close to victory.

That summer of 1989 we finally moved house from Harston to 28 Dunval Road, Bridgnorth, where we would stay for ten years. The kids found a nice new school and Rosie found work at the same school assisting children with special needs, a position that she still holds today.

As with many things in life, it wasn't quite as clear-cut as that, and later that year I made a bit of a return to playing. This would be the first of even more comebacks than Frank Sinatra ever made! Having not played for over a year, I was asked to play in a Pro-am at Little Lakes Golf Club in Bewdley and, unsurprisingly, I wasn't very good, taking 82. Then in October, Ram were running a French Pro-am at the superb Le Touquet Golf Club, and I was requested to play as Pro in a team. Although my form was far from great, I did just enough to want to play some more and in late October, played in two more Pro-ams at Northants County and the Belfry. I managed a 73 at Northants and brought in the winning team, getting much encouragement from my fellow Pros. At the very testing Belfry I scored a reasonable 78 and began to wonder if I may be able to compete again.

There was no simple answer to that notion. Looking back on the last 18 years since that time, I have occasionally been competitive as a professional, but mostly I have just made up the numbers with unpredictable performances. The lack of motor control and increasing lack of power has seriously hampered me. Changing to a belly-putter about three years ago seemed to improve my shaky putting and gave me a little more confidence.

1990-AGED 36

In 1990, with Ram's consent, I combined my job as a sales agent with a limited tournament schedule, representing the company, putting together 43 rounds in all. Without setting the world alight, I had several nice performances. In May I shot a fine four under par 67 in Shifnal's Pro-am to take first prize of £300 and, much as I hoped that this was the first of many good finishes, it was to be my best round of the year.

Another notable round was a one under par 67 in the pro-am at Mickleover. This was only one behind the winner and won £150. My brother Andrew, his university pal Matt Lofthouse and my old friend Richard Mobberley made up my team, on an enjoyable day. Big Matty, although directionally unpredictable, could hit some of the longest 6 irons I have ever seen! Mickleover had become one of my most successful venues, with a scoring average of 65.75 for four rounds on the par 68 track. The best of the four was my course record 63 from 1984. If all tournaments were held at Mickleover, I would have been a great champion!

In July, spurred on by a few good rounds, I had one more crack at The Open. It was to be at St. Andrews, and I was drawn at Ladybank for qualifying. I was able to stay with the Ram group, which reduced my expenses considerably, and the son of Mike Osborne, Ram's Sales Manager, was to caddy for me. I had practised hard, but was apprehensive about again playing in such classy company. On a perfect Scottish Sunday morning at 7.15, I was first to tee off in a field of 103. My misgivings about playing soon seemed justified as I rapidly dropped shots to be five over par after seven holes. Steadying down, I then had three close range birdie chances in a row, but missed them all. I would have just one more dropped shot coming in to finish on 77, six over par. I had only hit seven greens in regulation. All of the seven had been inside 15 feet, but I had been unable to convert any of those chances into birdies. With so many good players in the field, my chance of qualifying had all but gone, but I was determined to play better in the second round. Starting round two with a birdie, I was much improved throughout the front nine, reaching the turn in a one under par 35. Not quite so good coming home, a back nine of 38 would give me a 73, for a 36-hole total of 150. It was a respectable performance for me at the time, but it was way off the required standard to play in The Open. 139 was the qualifying score, eleven shots less than my effort, and I sensed this had been my final attempt at this great tournament.

The Open had been a passion of mine, ever since I first attended as an 18 year-old spectator at Birkdale in 1971. I had entered 15 times between 1972 and 1990, playing in the final qualifying competition 14 times. Successfully qualifying four times, I had escaped the 36-hole cut in each of those four Opens, and had made the 54-hole cut once, completing all four rounds in 1981 at Sandwich to finish 50th. All of my Opens-proper had been in England, although most of my qualifying rounds had been in Scotland. I had played 43 rounds in all stages and my stroke average was 74.5. My best round was 68 at Hillside in 1983 and my worst 84 at Lytham in 1979. It is a record I am proud of and undoubtedly some of my greatest golfing moments have been at The Open.

Trying to combine working for Ram with some playing, I managed a few decent rounds without winning much money and then came the 72-hole Midland Pro's Championship at the Forest of Arden in late August. In a tournament that I had threatened to win several times in the past, I would now be pleased just to make the cut with my present unpredictable form. Warm summer weather seemed to inspire me as I swung the club really well in the first round. Despite a lost ball on the seventh, four birdies helped me to a fine one under par 71 to be in sixth place. Day two didn't go so well and a 78 dropped me down the field, but was still good enough to make the cut. I was lucky enough to have Rosie caddying this week and round three began in spectacular style. After regulation pars on the first two holes I would make an amazing five consecutive birdies. The first four were long putts and the fifth a four-footer. After a mere par on the eighth to be five under par, I then proceeded to give all five shots back in the space of three holes! It would be 73 in the end, good, but not as good as it should have been. My last round was a mediocre 75 to put me in 18th position, a pleasing achievement considering the state I was in just a year earlier.

In September we had a Ram sales meeting at the Uckfield headquarters and finished with a competition at the superb East Sussex National, where the greens were super-quick even though the course was fairly new. Ram meetings were always scheduled near a good course and on other occasions we played Royal St. Georges and Sherwood Forest. Everyone was a golf-nut at Ram and they had quietly encouraged my return to playing.

There was to be one more notable tournament in 1990 and that was the Golf Plus PGA Four-Ball at Hillside and Hesketh in October. Renewing the old PGA Cup team partnership with Tony Minshall on two Southport courses where I had previously qualified for The Open seemed an ideal opportunity to regain some old form. It turned out to be a pleasant walk down memory lane as we combined well for an opening three under par 69 at Hillside. For round two we played the easier Hesketh and opened with a disappointing bogey five, but followed up with a blistering run of six birdies, four from me and two from Tony. Pars on eight and nine put us out in an amazing 29, five under par. Tony birdied the 10th, but then we bogeyed the short 11th. After a par on 12, Tony magnificently eagled the par-five 13th to take us to seven under par. Following scrambled pars on the next three, Tony birdied both the finishing par-fives to give us a nine under par 62, best round of the day! Lying fifth going into the final round, Hillside proved to be a stern test in an increasingly strong wind. Despite the conditions, we played a very solid front nine of 33, with six pars and three birdies. When Tony made a fine two-putt birdie four on the 11th, we must have been very close to the lead, but then things deteriorated in the gusty conditions. We finally came in with 71 for a 13 under par total of 202 to finish ninth and a prize of £370 each. It had been a lot of fun and we had both had spells of fine play. That would be my last competitive round for nearly six months. Since I was not attached to a club, I couldn't play in alliances, but it would not be long before I was again working at a club.

Over 43 rounds in the year I had averaged 74.5, and although I had not won much money, it seemed unbelievable that I was competing at all. How strange golf is, the way it drives you to despair, then lures you back into its grip.

1991–AGED 37

I was still with Ram when an article appeared in the Shropshire Star about a new golf course being built at Worfield, just outside Bridgnorth. I hadn't really intended to be a club pro again, but one thing led to another, and on May 1st I was Professional at Worfield Golf Club.

Although I had not played competitively over the winter, Professional friends such as Paul and Phil Hinton, Lee Bashford and Andy Arrowsmith had encouraged me with friendly games at local courses. When I did re-start my competitive schedule in the spring, I had a terrible time, scoring in the high 70's and low 80's. I would score no better than 72 in any round and would average 76.8 for 41 rounds throughout the year. I was slipping back into the mode of two years ago, but still believed there was some good golf to come, and practised hard for '92.

Being at Worfield had gone well. It had been fun to help set up a club and course from scratch, and the directors had used my knowledge and expertise to that end with some success. I had set up shop in a temporary building with the promise of a proper shop in a new clubhouse in the near future. Two local lads, Mike Phillips and Stuart Groves had joined me as assistants and we looked forward to a successful future at the club. Emily and Christopher had been given junior membership and were looking to get their first handicaps.

Although the dystonia was still there, it had improved since Gog Magog, and I was tentatively optimistic about my game. I had been given a sponsored Vauxhall car by the adjacent Worfield Garage, and was feeling more like a proper golf pro again.

1992–AGED 38

The new year's play got off to a much better start this time with several nice rounds in the alliances. The Shropshire and Herefordshire alliances, organised by Bridnorth pro Paul Hinton, included a pro's individual competition and for that reason, were much more interesting than the Warwickshire ones, which were purely better-ball. My most notable performance in these winter events was at Sapey Golf Club, where my 38 stableford points took first prize of £80. That two under par 67 was to be my best round of the year by four shots, and although I would record several good rounds throughout the year, it was hard to get excited about my play compared to the standard I had reached just six or seven years previously. In May I had organised a successful Pro-am at Worfield which attracted 36 teams. Everyone found the new course tough and scoring was high. Joe Higgins won the pro's section with a 73 and my 77 came in third. My team came in fourth on what turned out to be an excellent day.

Things were going well in our life when, for the first time we were to be affected by crime. After a few days away visiting relatives, we returned home to find our front door open and discovered that we had been burgled. We didn't own much of value, but they took all they could find, such as Rosie's jewellery, cameras, video and worst of all, cash out of Emily's money-box. This was all quite upsetting, but worse was to come. Ten days later, my shop at Worfield was comprehensively burgled in a raid where most of the stock was taken. Less than a month later, just when I was recovering from this, with the lost stock replaced, the shop was again hit in a night raid. Thirteen days later, yet another night-time burglary on the shop would be the last straw. My insurance company, and all the others, refused future cover in the temporary building which housed my shop. There seemed no imminent prospect of a clubhouse, and since I was unwilling to re-stock the vulnerable shop with uninsured goods, Worfield Golf Club and I parted company. It was sad to go, having helped the club to grow and it has been pleasing to see the course develop so well in the years that followed.

As one might expect, my game was at best mediocre in the remainder of 1992, as I tried to pull myself together. In 37 rounds I had averaged 76.3 and won about £1,000. This was to be the last year in which my winnings would reach four figures. The glory days were well and truly gone.

12

REFLECTIONS

I would have a few decent rounds in subsequent years, the best of which was a four under par 66 at Oswestry in the Shropshire and Herefordshire Open of 1996, but mostly I would just make up the numbers. By 2003 I had reached the pleasing total of 100 competitive rounds in the sixties, but low scores had become scarce by this time. In 2001 I had my eighth hole-in-one at Bude Golf Club on the fourth hole. This was 33 years after my first at Moortown. I'm still trying for more! I had that albatross two on the par-five tenth at Muthaiga in 1973, and lots of twos on par-fours, but the best shot I ever holed? It would have to be that 1 iron to the elevated fourth green at Sunningdale New for an eagle two in 1980.

My golf career took various different paths after Worfield from club pro to sales agent to teaching pro, and it has been in the final role of golf coach that I have concentrated on over the last few years at Horsehay Golf Centre in Telford.

Looking back at the time when I was a serious player, between 1972 and 1986, I have tried to come up with the people who had the most influence on my golf. Technically speaking, Bill Miller was my main mentor. From when I first joined him as assistant in 1969, throughout my most successful period I would periodically make visits to Fairhaven for swing checks. Bill had been heavily influenced

Rosie on the bag at Telford Golf Hotel, Shropshire, 1998.

by Ben Hogan in his early years and Hogan's "Modern fundamentals of golf", first published in 1957, was a regular subject for discussion in the Fairhaven shop. When the 'square-to-square' theory appeared in the late 60's, we worked hard to incorporate it into our swings, but Bill's conclusion, with which I would now agree, was that while there was merit in all these methods, you had to develop your own way of swinging the club and stick with it.

Bill's story turned out to be very sad in the end. Coming to Fairhaven from the Cardross club of Glasgow in 1968 as a recent Scottish Professional champion, his fresh approach at the club was quite radical. In his newly built shop, he stocked a wide selection of clothing as well as clubs, and our smart establishment was highly regarded in the area. Although a keen student of the golf swing, yips trouble curtailed his play and he was rarely seen on the course, a great shame for someone in his early thirties. Bill's wife Sadie was a keen helper in the shop, and their only child, Gary, would turn into a fine golfer in his own right. Bill unfortunately developed a debilitating illness, which seemed to age him prematurely and then, tragically, Sadie died of a brain tumour. Just a few years later Bill himself passed away, and finally, Gary's life ended at a terribly young age.

The other main influences in the development of my game would be John Jacobs, Jack Nicklaus and Martin Hall. John probably gave me no more than four lessons, but I avidly took in every wise word of advice and his book "Practical Golf" would be a text-book for me. While a junior at Moortown Golf Club in 1969, I was an interested bystander during the filming of John's Yorkshire Television series "Play Better Golf". I could understand his simple methods of analysing the ball flight His concept of the shoulders turning while the arms have a free swing was one that I have always fallen back on. He could always cut through the mystique of how the club hit the ball in the days before high-speed photography showed us exactly what happened.

Jack Nicklaus helped me in a different way. Firstly, as a young boy I used to watch him in awe playing in TV matches with Gary Player and Arnold Palmer in "Big Three Golf". Then seeing him in person for the first time at Royal Birkdale in the 1969 Ryder Cup,

I was amazed at the power and control of his shots. His 1974 book "Golf My Way" was instrumental in my swing development. Before Tiger Woods came along, Jack was certainly the greatest player of all time.

Martin Hall was a contemporary of mine who was an excellent prospect as a young player, but decided at a relatively young age to concentrate on teaching. He assisted some of the top American coaches and had already picked up a lot of new ideas when I first consulted him at Trentham Golf Club in the early 80's. I would make several trips to see Martin in that period and found his advice invaluable. He moved to the USA soon after and has become one of their highest rated teachers.

Many fine golf tutors have come through in subsequent years, and two in particular stand out for me. First David Leadbetter who, after becoming famous as Nick Faldo's mentor, became one of the best at describing the feelings of a good swing. You need good mental images in that second or so that it takes to hit the ball. My other choice would be American Jim Mclean, who advocates working towards finding certain positions at different stages in the swing, while accepting that small deviations from these ideals can still work. These are concepts that I use in my own teaching.

My other main influence and source of encouragement has been my wonderful wife Rosie. From when she first came to see what this pro golf playing was all about at Redditch in 1975 to the present day she has supported, cajoled and consoled me through my many ups and downs on the course. Through her caddying role, we have shared many great times on the course- 1978 at Oxley Park, when my 65 broke the course record that had stood for 30 years by three shots. The 1980 PGA Cup in Oklahoma where we shared the excitement of international match-play. Plus numerous other occasions when she has kept me going through patches of despondency.

Younger brother Andrew and I also shared unforgettable times in the four Open Championships and other tournaments in which he caddied for me. Having somebody familiar to talk to, who understood my game was always a calming influence in the midst of all the excitement and pressure, even though he says I was grumpy on the course! We made a great team, and while Andrew is a fine player in his own right, business commitments have, thus-far, prevented his full development as a golfer. It was disappointing that Emily and Christopher were too young to have witnessed my successful times on the course, but in the mid-nineties, when in their teens, we did play a lot of golf together, and I hope in the future they will get some enjoyment out of the game.

Since my tournament career ended in the mid-80's there have been some big changes in the way that top-class golf is played. The equipment is now so much better, the balls we use now are incredible. They spin like the old balatas, but fly as far, if not farther than the old solid balls, and they don't cut! The big-headed titanium drivers with the latest generation of graphite shafts are so much easier to hit than the Hogan persimmon driver with steel shaft that I used throughout most of my best years. When you put the new driver and the new ball in the hands of a good player, the results are amazing. In the 70's and 80's a drive of 250 yards was pretty long and the only way of driving 300 yards was with the assistance of a following wind and firm ground. These days you could add 50 yards to those two statements and that would be a fair assessment of good players' drives! On tour, players who drive less than 280 yards are considered short, and in The Open we are now regularly seeing 400 yard tee-shots!

All this means that there are now very few true par-fives for top players and courses have had to be made ever longer in order to test them. It seems wrong that most of our famous old courses, such as Sunningdale and St. Enodoc are now considered too short for the elite golfers. I firmly believe it is about time a 'tournament' ball, with reduced distance, was introduced. This would allow a 6,500 yard course to again be challenging for all players.

The other major event in world golf over the last decade or so has been the emergence of Tiger Woods. I first saw him as a raw 19 year-old amateur in the 1995 Walker Cup at Royal Porthcawl. He seemed to hit the ball miles, but without much control, and while one sensed a phenomenal talent, the finished article was clearly not yet there. Since then, his improvement has been relentless and he seems well on target to overtake Jack Nicklaus's total of 18 majors. A strong argument could be made already that Tiger is the greatest player of all time, even though I think he may still have his best years to come. I have been lucky enough to see him play in person a number of times, the most memorable of which was in the final round of the 1998 Open at Birkdale. With my then 15 year-old son Christopher, we went all the way round with Tiger to witness an amazing round of 66, which left him just one shot behind champion Mark O'Meara and Brian Watts, who lost in a play-off.

Trying to draw conclusions is not easy, but having written this book, I now feel in a better position to do so. As a teenager, I was a very talented young player, and having made rapid progress, I was slowed somewhat by turning professional prematurely. Eventually reaching the standard of the other pros by my early twenties, I came very close to breaking into the big time, and when I did share the stage with star players I usually gave a good account of myself. I could be a streaky player and, when on a roll would produce some low numbers, borne out by the twenty or so course records I set or equalled.

From my mid-twenties the dreaded dystonia began to get hold of me, but I think my greatest achievement in the game was to compete successfully for several more years despite that. I like to imagine that without the neurological condition I would have got to the top level in the game, but who knows? Maybe other problems would have stopped me, such as the back problems I have suffered for some time. I hope that my determination to battle on through adversity may inspire others to do the same, not only in sport but in all walks of life. Although most of my rounds these days are disappointing, I still enjoy playing a good course in nice condition, and from time to time put a decent score together, but can't help thinking back to those days when I competed with the best.

POSTSCRIPT

A proud son.

Reading the history of my Dad's golfing career has brought a great deal of clarity to my own memories of stories told and times gone by.

I remember going along to clubs in and around Bridgnorth with Dad and being amazed at how many people knew him and recognised him – and feeling their gaze as I tried to fumble my way around the course without getting in anyone's way. Golf is without doubt one of the most difficult sports in world, and one for which skills are not inherited. At least not in my case anyway.

One moment stands out for me as a turning point in my recognition of Dad's achievements. I forget which one, but he was playing in a local pro tournament which was won by his close friend Paul Hinton. Afterwards Paul was congratulated by a passer by as we talked to him with a group of local pros. His humility prevailed, and rather than graciously accepting the praise all he could do was say that it didn't mean anything – in the old days it was David Thorp that was the real local star with achievements far in excess of his own.

Despite my Dad's own downbeat view of his game, it still takes quite a player to chase him around a good golf course. Even with his shakes and aches, I never fail to be impressed with the accuracy and concentration in his game.

Working on this book, I have learned in detail the highs and lows of Dad's career and I hope you have found the journey just as fascinating.

I only wish I had been around to cheer him along from the galleries, but playing with him today it's still clear that while the competitive days are over, there's more than a hint of the old desire to win in every swing.

ACKNOWLEDGEMENTS

Express & Star

The Birmingham Post

Blackpool Gazette

Cambridge Evening News

PGA

R&A

THANKS TO

Christopher, Emily and Rosie.

Printed in the United Kingdom
by Lightning Source UK Ltd.
131012UK00002B/79-150/P